Behind the Eyes of Liberty Pearl

by

WENDY DALE YOUNG

ISBN-13: 978-1726302760 (paperback)
ISBN-10: 1726302768 (paperback)

On March 20, 2003 missiles detonated Saddam Hussein's Presidential Palace in Baghdad. From the rubble, U. S. Marines rescued a small white puppy. Her story is told by her best friend Savannah and Liberty Pearl herself.

Dedicated to my parents, Gini and Angus and to all the brave men and woman who defend our country. Thank you.

Acknowledgements

Special thanks to Deborah Hand-Cutler and Richard Laurence for reading early drafts and offering suggestions.

Thank you so much for photo courtesy:
Title photo, "Liberty Pearl" Angela Murray Boles.

Back cover, "Wendy & Liberty Pearl" by Angela Murray Boles.

Page 79 "Savannah & Liberty Pearl" by PetCo.

Page 115, 167 "Chewey" by Lisa Young, CEO of rescue group "The Rescue Train."

Page 119, "Jasper" by Heather Lipson Bell.

Page 120, "Kevin" and "Josh & Cathy" by Scott Nicolaides.

Page 165, "Libby & Sam" by Angela Murray Boles.

All other photos by Wendy Dale Young

Foreword

by Marcy Christmas
Marcy rescued Liberty Pearl from Iraq.

Getting a dog out of Iraq is not an easy thing to do. Liberty Pearl came out in the back of a van filled with dogs. These had been chosen by soldiers who managed to take them to the Baghdad Zoo where we had been collecting them. These lucky dogs were going to the soldiers' families in the United States. Now in the van, they were making the journey across the desert to Amman, Jordan.

At the Humane Center for Animal Welfare in Amman, a shelter run by an English couple, the dogs and a few cats were spayed or neutered, and then received their shots. Even on the 10-hour journey to Amman, and during their surgeries, the animals never whimpered. They knew something very big was happening to them, and the people around them were so very kind.

Liberty Pearl flew inside a crate with Colonel Susan's dog. The plane was delayed, so we were very anxious as we waited at the Los Angeles International Airport. It was late at night. When Liberty Pearl and the Colonel's dog finally arrived, Suzie stopped at a fast-food restaurant, thinking they must be hungry. I tried to explain my experience with Iraqi dogs — they don't eat meat or <u>any</u> dog food, only bread and plants. That was their diet.

Colonel Suzie originally called "Liberty Pearl" "Pelican," because she had been in a cage with a friendly pelican at the zoo. I called her "Quiet" because she never made a sound. She just ran for cover whenever <u>any</u> sound was made. In my backyard she hid under a bush. **This dog was not what anyone would call a "pet."** I was busy getting other soldier's dogs out of Iraq, so I asked my friend Wendy if she could assess "Quiet" and give an opinion as to her behavior, in other words could she be rehabilitated. Wendy has far more patience than I have. Wendy took this shell-shocked puppy, renamed her "Liberty Pearl," and with extraordinary patience and a lot of love Wendy turned Liberty Pearl back into a real wonderful dog. She takes loud noises perfectly in stride now, and she looks after rescued birds, kittens and dogs just as she was treasured and taught by Wendy's large dog Savannah.

Wendy is a hero. The four-legged and the winged all benefit from her presence. I couldn't have done what she did, and I consider myself lucky to have had her in my life. Bravo Wendy!

Marcy Christmas
October 11, 2017

Introduction

Savannah Meets Liberty Pearl

When I first met Liberty Pearl, she looked as if she came out of a tumble-dry, not-so-gentle cycle. Her hair was frizzy with static. One of her eyes had a serious Marty Feldman stare. She sat in a little dog crate, frozen in a pose resembling a delicate glass-blown figurine. If she dared move, I thought she might shatter into a million pieces.

I never smelled anything like that before. The immense pain and fear sweating through the little dog's paws was overwhelming. My alpha female self immediately melted into a passionate, overbearing mother with only one sensation in my heart and one mission to accomplish.

In the spring of 2004, I had just turned thirteen, a ripe ol' age for a Gordan Setter. After chasing trillions of tennis balls, running in parks across the San Fernando Valley, hiking in Laurel Canyon, meeting and rescuing kitties and birds everywhere, I was ready for a calmer, less physical life.

In an instant, my new role was in front of my nose, and it wasn't a squirrel to chase up a tree. My job was to enable that little angel pup to find her wings, play, eat, pee, and be happy being a dog. My tail wagged like a puppy at her first day of doggie daycare.

My mission began. I adopted Saddam Hussein's daughters' dog into my home and straight into my heart.

Savannah

1

Nightmare in the Baghdad Palace

March 20, 2003. It was like any other Thursday. There had been a nice rain in the morning leaving the air crisp and clean. The temperature was a perfect 73 degrees. I woke up that morning after a long peaceful sleep. It was very still in the Palace.

I heard the familiar traffic in the distance and the birds singing in the trees just outside. I was hungry and thirsty. I made my way down the big staircase. It wasn't easy. I was only a four- pound puppy! I couldn't really step down the stairs so I "plopped" my way down, falling a few times. It was kind of fun. It was much easier going down the stairs than it will be going back up. I'll worry about getting back up later. Right now, I need to eat.

I had a long empty hallway ahead of me. The floor was hard, cold and slippery. My paws shot out from under me a few times and I lost my balance. After what seemed to be a mile walk I sniffed my way into the kitchen. I did this journey the past two days, so I had it down. There were a few bowls of water and bowls full of rice. I missed my scraps of goodies that the girls sometimes gave me, but this would do.

The only difference this day was that I was all by myself. My people had left a couple days ago. I don't know where they went. I was becoming more and more anxious being alone.

After I had my breakfast I began to investigate, sniffing up and down the long echoing hallways and large majestic rooms. I'd never been allowed down these halls or in these rooms. Again, the floors were slick, so I slipped a lot.

There was a lot to inspect but nothing seemed all that exciting. I began to feel empty, a little scared. I didn't like being alone. I needed to relieve myself. Usually a man with long thick smelly gloves would fetch me and take me outside to do my business. I didn't like him. He was called a "handler." He wasn't very nice to me. He'd pick me up roughly and hold me in the air far away from his body.

The "handler" would be responsible for me off and on during each day. But he wasn't here either on this day. So yesterday I chose a spot in one of the rooms to "pay my visits." I finished what I needed to do and was done with investigating.

Feeling tired I laid down on the cold marble floor by the main door ready to greet my girls when they came home. I sniffed at the door all day, waiting. Surely, they're coming back.

I was feeling very lonely. I was used to the girls fussing over me. I loved the attention and the warmth of their arms around me, although I really don't like being held. I pretended I liked it for maybe a minute or so. But I would welcome it now.

Normally I was kept in a caged pen. They said it was for my own safety. But now I had the whole place to myself. It was dead quiet in my Palace. There was nothing else to do but sleep. I was good at that. Especially because I was a very young puppy.

I woke up mid-afternoon. I walked to the kitchen and drank some more water and munched on more rice. I decided to tackle the staircase to lie on my warm comfortable bed. This was good exercise for me, stretching and pulling myself up the challenging marble stairs. I had a couple of tumbles but finally reached the top.

I was too little to jump onto the bed, so the girls always left a stool by the side of the bed for me. After a few attempts I was on the stool and crawled up to the bed. Against the cozy pillows I dug at the soft, smooth sheets, burrowing a little spot for me to fit into. Finally satisfied I curled up.

A pillow fell on top of me. I felt comfortable but a little uneasy. I worried about my girls. I kept hoping they would come bounding into our room and pick me up and kiss me all over. I began to tremble. It was getting dark and I was alone. I couldn't help but whimper. Where is everyone?

I sniffed the air. There was a scent of rain. The drops were hitting the windows making a gentle rhythm against the panes. It calmed me a little. My eyes grew heavy. I fell asleep.

I was in a deep slumber. I was dreaming. My feet began to twitch. I felt like I was running. I felt a vibration underneath me as if someone was walking past the bed. Could it be? The girls are home? I was still in a deep sleep.

Suddenly a horribly high-pitched siren sound pierced my ears. Ouch! Wait. My ears hurt so much I thought my head would explode. Am I dreaming? No, this is real. And there wasn't anyone walking by the bed.

I woke up frozen with fear. The vibration I felt now began moving my bed. The ceiling, walls and ground were shaking. It sounded like a train was barreling through the Palace. The horribly high-pitched, now blood-curling siren sound rumbled louder and deeper.

Then BAM! Within seconds, I heard a huge explosion on the other side of the Palace. Holes were ripped through the ceiling and walls. Marble, cement, gold and chandeliers were falling all around me. Fire and smoke shot up high into the sky. There were lightning bolts of flashing lights everywhere.

The pillow that had been over me flew away and I was being tossed about on the bed like a ping-pong ball. The air was black and thick. I felt like a tidal wave of dirt had engulfed me. I couldn't see anything. I couldn't hear anything but the ringing in my ears. My head ached. I breathed in the thick mist. I couldn't smell anything. My nose was filled with dust and debris. I began to cough. It was hard to breath. My eyes were stinging. I was terrified. I knew I had to run. But where?

The walls and ceiling continued to drop down all around me. I was thrown off the bed. I landed on a slab of marble. I slid off and tried to move. I couldn't walk as there was so much debris, so I crawled. I didn't know where I was going but I had to get out. It was pitch black. I had to rely on my scent, but I was so congested I couldn't get a good sense of where I was.

Then I fell through a hole where the floor had disappeared. I landed on one of the stairs. But there were no other stairs to go to. Half of the staircase was missing. I was stuck. I was frantic. There was another loud rumble and I was flung out into the air. Magically I landed on the pillow that had covered me. I think I was close to the ground floor now. And I think there was a Guardian angel looking after me.

I felt a breeze against my face, so I decided to follow that. It was still pitch black. Fire was raging all down the hallways. The heat from the fire was absorbed in the rubble and dust surrounding me. From the firelight I was able to see a large gap near the main doors leading to the outside. My heart was pounding so hard. Could I make it to the opening? I had to, or I would suffocate.

Terrified, I crawled until I was almost at the opening. I began to breathe easier. Then suddenly, that same horribly high-pitched blood curling siren of a sound filled the space. It was descending, and the ground began to shake with a horrible roar. Hysterically I began to burrow. There had to be some way of getting out!

That train was rumbling through the Palace again. BAM! Another explosion. I began to cry, screaming at the top of my lungs.

Then something very hard fell on my head. I saw stars. My head hurt. It hurt so much. Liquid ran down my face into my mouth. It tasted bitter. The hot, thick, black mist filled the air and my lungs again. I coughed. Each cough made my head throb even more. I was shaking uncontrollably. Fire was crackling closer to me. Where are my girls? What is happening. Help! I saw stars again. I blacked out.

I woke up to the sound of voices. I must have been asleep for hours. Maybe days? Sunlight filled the detonated ruined Palace. Small fires still crackled, and the air had a mean stale stench.

The voices were coming closer. I tried to lift my head to see what was going on, but I couldn't move. Debris covered me. I cried. What else could I do. I was injured and covered by cement, marble and chunks of gold.

The voices were very close now. The people were entering my home. I cried louder. Maybe someone will hear me. I was hoarse, my throat coated with dust and debris. But I kept crying. I couldn't stop. I was shaking so much that the dirt from the debris was falling all around me. The more I cried the more my head throbbed. But I had to keep crying. Surely somebody will hear me.

Then I heard shouts. The shouts were coming closer. My heart was pounding so loud that I thought someone may hear it! I didn't understand the talking, it was not what I was used to. My whimpers for help were stifled now. I wore my voice out. I couldn't bark. Will anyone find me?

"Look! Look over there to your left" a voice yelled. "That pile of rubble. Something is sticking out under that block of marble." They were looking for survivors or bodies.

Suddenly there were two booted feet in front of my nose. "Oh, my God! It's a little gray dog!" I was so filthy they didn't know I was actually pure white. The man lifted the large chunk of marble off from me. There were two other large slabs that the marble chunk had fallen on top of, protecting me otherwise I would have been crushed.

"C'mon little pup, everything is okay. You're safe now."

He yelled to the others, "Looks like her head was hit pretty bad, there's blood everywhere."

How'd he know I was a she? I didn't care just as long as they found me. Gently he lifted me up and took me into his arms. There were oohs and aahs coming from all the men. I later learned that these men were called "marines" and were known to be tough. But they were kind to me.

As ill as I felt and as little as I like to be held, especially by a man, I was relieved. I felt these people were here to help me. And they weren't wearing long, thick smelly gloves. The Marine kissed me and tried to move the bloody hair from my eyes. He carried me to a truck.

"I'll take this little one to the zoo myself" he told the driver.

And off we went.

There were nice people waiting for me at the zoo. The zoo housed all the surviving wild animals after it was bombed. It became the home for several stray dogs that the Marines fell in love with and wanted to keep safe. As my Marine handed me to a young woman he told her that I came from the Baghdad Presidential Palace and that I must have been one of the daughters' pup.

"Can't imagine Hussein loving on this sweet li'l puppy." He said he would check in on me later.

The nice young woman took me to a room.

"There, there" she said "I'll take good care of you. Let's wash your head and see what happened."

Gently she washed the grim and blood from my head. Ouch! It hurt. I was shaking from head to toe. I was scared out of my mind. But I was feeling so weak that I had no choice but to let her help me. The warm water started to feel soothing, but my head was aching something awful. She cleaned my ears and my nostrils as best she could.

"You have quite a cut on your head little one. We're going to have to keep a close eye on you as I think you sustained a concussion. Your right eye is a little off."

She dried me off while giving me kisses.

"You're going to sleep with me tonight. Please stop shaking. Don't be scared."

I continued to tremble and shiver for most of my stay while I was residing at the zoo, which would be eight long months. Another nice young woman named Colonel Susan took a real liking to me and visited me every day. She gave me treats from her MRE meals. I liked that. Colonel Susan and others worried that I may not make it as I was so shell shocked. They thought the stress alone could kill me.

But I surprised them. I had a strong will and determination. I didn't think I will ever get through the trauma that I lived through that final night in the Palace. I refused to eat most of the time, except for Colonel Susan's treats. I stayed only four to five pounds for the next year.

Once the nice young woman and Colonel Susan thought I was healthy enough to live in the zoo on my own, they placed me in a cell with a tamed Pelican. My name became Pelican 2. Pelican 1 became my new best friend. He let me snuggle with him.

My favorite place to sit was right under a leaky faucet. The cool, soft drops felt good during those scorching hot days. The drops of water joined my tears dancing down my face. This was the safest place to be. For now. But I wondered. This can't be it. Where are my girls? And where do I go from here?

2

Sweet America

Hi. My name is Savannah and I'm here to help li'l Liberty Pearl explain her story.

It started with a phone call. On December 15, 2003, Marcy Christmas called Wendy, my mom and guardian. Marcy was the main rescuer responsible for Liberty Pearl's escape. Could we meet her at LAX the next day? She was picking up three dogs from Iraq, one of which was Saddam Hussein's dog who she was taking home with her. Marcy had named the puppy "Quiet" when they met. Regretfully, we had to work, so we'd miss out on that exciting greeting, but we couldn't wait to meet her.

Her homecoming was anything but harmonious. The poor little thing was petrified. Marcy was gravely concerned. Quiet trembled uncontrollably and hid whenever she could. She suffered from serious post-traumatic syndrome disorder. Liberty Pearl later told me that her favorite hiding spot was outside behind a large bougainvillea bush in the backyard.

Marcy had a heck of a time getting her back into the house. Once she did, the moment the door opened, Quiet bolted right back for the safety of her bush. Marcy lived near an airport, so when a plane flew overhead, or even worse, when the garbage trucks made their growling weekly route down the street, Quiet went berserk.

"It was too close to home," Liberty Pearl told me, "reminders of the missiles imploding the Presidential Palace or the constant bombings while I was living in the Baghdad Zoo."

Not knowing where to hide, she ran in circles from one place to another, panting like she'd just finished a ten-mile marathon.

She always found her way back to her bougainvillea bush. That was her comfort spot. She was constantly cowering, and, as she did in Iraq, she rolled onto her back with her legs in the air and an expression that said, "Step on me. Get it over with."

Marcy lives in Camarillo, about an hour's drive from our home in Studio City. We wanted to drive out to meet Quiet, but Marcy was extremely protective and felt the pup needed more time to settle in, at least until she stopped shaking. Marcy spent all her free time with Quiet. Marcy rescued Chihuahuas, too, and had six in her home during Quiet's stay.

"The pups gave me some comfort, but the bougainvillea bush was my main shelter," Liberty Pearl told me.

🐾

Four months passed. Quiet calmed down a little. She allowed Marcy to rub her tummy but only for a minute. She found some refuge under the couch, but she still had her drill of running in circles and bolting to the bush whenever the garbage trucks rolled by.

"I thought we were under attack!" she told me. "The rumbles were terrifying."

She started to eat better, although it took several months before Marcy could get her used to dog food. There was no dog food in Iraq.

"At first, I walked away from it, and I only ate the rice and bread in my dish," she told me. "That was what I was used to."

After a few weeks, Marcy's backyard looked like it had been vandalized. Most of her plants, grass, and anything else that was green had been eaten. At first, Marcy thought it was rabbits, but she soon discovered it was Quiet. The dog was finding her minerals and nutrients. When she finally decided she liked dog food, she felt much better.

At one point, Marcy had a realtor come to her house as a courtesy, to tell her the value of her home. The Realtor saw Quiet and fell in love with the terrified pup. Marcy told us the lady wanted her and promised to take Quiet to work with her. Her coworkers would ooh and aah over Saddam Hussein's dog, she said.

But Marcy was protective. If everyone knows she's Hussein's dog, she'll never have any peace. She should be with someone who'll let her be a dog.

Marcy turned the Realtor down. It was another two months before we met Quiet.

One day, Marcy called to tell us she had a Chihuahua that had been mistreated. The previous owner had hit her over the head and left the little dog traumatized with seizures. Since 1995, Wendy had been with a professional dance company called Bethune Theatredanse, where she worked as an instructor of Performing Arts for special-needs children and adults.

Since Wendy worked with these special people, Marcy thought we might like to have the Chihuahua. If we couldn't take her, maybe Wendy's mother, Gini, might want her. Wendy made a deal with Marcy.

"If you bring the Chihuahua to meet us, you have to bring Quiet, too," Wendy said. "We're dying to meet her."

Wendy had a feeling about Quiet. When Marcy originally called to meet her at LAX to pick up Quiet, Wendy had an epiphany. Some would call it voices in her head, but she received a sign about Quiet.

Wendy and I were on our afternoon walk when a voice spoke to her and said, "You need to help a little white dog."

At first, she thought that meant our friend Michelle's little Maltese, Tommy, who was in grave condition.

"You mean a little boy?" Wendy asked the voice.

"No. It's a little girl dog."

She didn't think much more about it, assuming the message had gotten crossed with Tommy. It wasn't until we took in Quiet that we realized she was the one we were supposed to help.

3
Homecoming

On June 8, 2004 Marcy arrived at our house with two crates. I thought I would burst with anticipation. I was like a kid on Christmas morning and I couldn't wait to open that little gift wrapped in a beige crate. Marcy set the two crates on the floor and opened the small pink one. Out came a tiny Chihuahua, shaking a little.

Marcy picked her up to introduce us. "This is Petunia."

I said hello to Petunia, but I was still being pulled toward the other crate and what it contained.

Marcy handed Petunia to Wendy, and she held the tiny tyke in her hands and kissed her head. Feeling her trembling, Wendy held her close to her heart and stroked her gently, as she sat on the couch.

I eyed the unopened crate the whole time we sat and chatted. Petunia soon calmed down and fell asleep on Wendy's lap.

When do I get to meet Quiet? I wondered.

I could hardly stand it. I was much more interested in

the second crate, circling it occasionally and sniffing the front door. No sound came from inside.

I was about to speak up and bark to say the second gift needed to be opened, when Marcy asked, "Are you ready to meet Quiet?"

Am I ever!

Wendy handed Petunia to Marcy, who bent down to open the magical crate. I stood behind her while the door opened.

There she was. I never saw a sadder, more-traumatized face in my life. Quiet's right eye was a little off, having survived a concussion when the bombs hit the Palace. Her walleye made her look even more devastated, and she had tear stains under both eyes. Her thin, wispy hair stood out like it was filled with static cling.

I gasped and froze. Suddenly, Quiet lay down and flipped onto her back with her head outside the crate, her legs and paws in the air. She seemed to be saying, "Hurry up. Step on me and get it over with."

She was totally silent. Sensing her fear, I went to the crate to sniff Quiet's head, then I licked her tear-stained face. Quiet didn't move and didn't even seem to be breathing.

Like a puppy at doggie day care, I stepped back and did my best "down dog" pose, flipping my paws and legs backward. I repeated the playful motion a couple times, trying to encourage Quiet and let her know she was welcome and to please come out to meet us.

She didn't budge. I gave her face a couple more loving licks, nosing her to turn over and come out.

"I'm petrified," Quiet said. "Where am I?"

"You're safe, little One. It's all right. My name is Savannah."

She must have felt the love I offered. The next move happened so fast, it was a blur. Quiet stood with her nose pointed at my face, looking me straight in the eye, then bolted out of the crate and ran off at full speed. I followed like a proud mare with a newborn foal.

We romped through our little apartment like it was the grassiest, largest, most-open pasture we ever saw. Marcy and Wendy were aghast, watching our glee for several minutes.

Occasionally, Quiet stopped and rolled onto her back for a few seconds. I sniffed her all over from head to foot and finished by licking her face. Up she went and ran off again.

Marcy explained that Quiet liked and was used to big dogs, because most dogs in Iraq were medium to large.

When Quiet was in the Baghdad Zoo, her cellmate was a tame pelican. There were several stray dogs boarded there. Saddam's son's German Shepherd was in the zoo, along with a dog named Lucky. Quiet and Lucky became fast friends.

While the dogs were being boarded at the zoo, sometimes a few fortunate ones including Quiet, Lucky, and the Shepherd were taken on outings to the Presidential

Palace, where a unit of soldiers was stationed. The premises included a large swimming pool, where the dogs had a luxurious swim to cool off from the arid desert summer. Quiet loved being with bigger dogs. She followed them around like a lamb followed its flock.

"They gave me protection and understood me," she said.

Quiet and I finally settled down, and she found her new position. She lay inside my front legs, nestled against my chest. Her face still had a look of total sadness, but her forehead wasn't as furled. She was clearly more relaxed.

"Savannah, I feel safe and secure with you, but what happens now? I don't want to go back into the crate," she told me.

Before I could reply, Marcy asked, "Well, Wen? How about taking Quiet for her first walk?"

Wendy had collars and leashes ready for Petunia and Quiet. It was a small investment she made, subconsciously knowing we would keep Quiet.

Wendy began harnessing Quiet. She looked up into Wendy's face and saw love in her eyes.

"What a kind face," Quiet thought. "What's this around my neck? I'll be taken away now, right? I can't go back."

Quiet sat down.

"OK, Guys, let's go pay visits," Wendy told us, using the expression she'd been raised with from her childhood in England.

The door opened, and I was on my way out, eager to

show Quiet everything outside until I realized she wasn't with me. I turned and went back to her, licking her face and turning back toward the door.

Quiet looked up and asked softly, "I'm scared Savannah. Do we have to go?"

"Yes. We're going to do one of my favorite things. You are going to love it. C'mon."

Quiet joined me in perfect sync, and we walked through the door together and down the stairs to a new adventure.

We lived in Studio City near the main street, called Tujunga Avenue. Wendy was raised a half mile from that house. We had lovely residential streets. I turned right outside the apartment gate to take us up Elmo Avenue. Marcy and Wendy let me take the lead. I didn't always wear a leash.

Quiet was keeping up, but her tail was tucked firmly between her legs, and she shook uncontrollably.

"I don't think I can do this. I don't know the smells. I'm confused."

"Trust me," I told her. "I won't let anything happen to you."

I constantly kept turning around to make sure my new little buddy was with me. Quiet shot under me as if finding a sacred refuge. My heart ached for her. I managed to do my business, even with my little friend straddling between my legs. I'm a girl, but I must've had a lot of tomboy in me, because I liked to pee like a guy. I shimmied up to a tree or bush and lifted my leg.

Even on the grass, I lifted my leg. Occasionally, I

squatted. On that walk, I did more squatting than usual, hoping to demonstrate the technique to Quiet. Her body language said, *Get me out of here!*

"This isn't what I'm used to. This green stuff has a lot of different smells and lots of dog odors on it. Can I pee on it?" she asked me.

There was very little grass in Iraq, so the dogs were used to concrete on the Palace premises and while living at the zoo. Walking and peeing on grass would be a first for Quiet.

Wendy held tightly to the leash, as Quiet pulled. She feared Quiet would bolt away from us. A neighbor in front of us up the street walked out from his driveway.

Quiet froze. "Who's that? I don't like this."

She hid under me, and we couldn't get her to budge. She shook uncontrollably.

"I can't go on. I want to go back to the apartment where it's safe."

Wendy reached to pick her up, but she squirmed away and then lay on her back, taking the "ready to die" position. Wendy managed to lift Quiet, and we decided that was enough for the moment. Wendy and I were close to tears, holding that precious, shell-shocked pup, who was clearly terrified.

We went back to the apartment. Quiet gathered herself again while resting against my chest. Once she stopped shaking, I explained we needed to go out again, but in a car, another of my favorite things. I assured her we did it every day, and she'd like it.

"As long as you're with me," she said.

We loaded up and went to visit Wendy's mom, Gini, at her condo. We had a deal with Marcy to introduce Petunia to Gini.

We arrived at Gini's and were greeted by her fourteen-year-old poodle, Beau; Minxie; a one-eyed beautiful Tortie-Calico kitty and Sterling; a handsome tuxedo kitty who we called the "Cary Grant" of all kitties. He was very debonair. They looked at Quiet for a moment. Minxie and Sterling went back to their nap, and Beau came up to sniff Quiet and give her a kiss.

"That's nice," Quiet said, but she stayed under me.

Gini made tea, as we made introductions. Beau didn't seem at all interested in Petunia. We were concerned it would be too much for Gini to have a second dog with three pets already in the house.

While sitting on the couch, Petunia had a seizure and began biting the air, then at Wendy. Marcy realized it was too much stimulation. Petunia needed a one-on-one person who could give her all the love and affection she deserved.

As we left Gini's to drive back to our apartment, Marcy asked, "Do you want to keep Quiet for a couple nights and see how it goes?"

Did we? I wondered. *Does a cat wear pajamas?*

"Did you hear that, Quiet? You'll stay with us!"

She sighed in exhausted relief.

On Marcy's way out, we thought we'd give Quiet another chance to pay visits. She hadn't peed since early morning. The same thing happened. She didn't want to walk on the street. Defeated, we returned to our flat.

Marcy left with Petunia. Quiet noticed the empty crate in Marcy's hand and looked up at me.

"I'm really staying here? The crate's leaving without me?"

She stopped shaking so much.

It was dinnertime, so Wendy put out dinners for our three kitties—Maxamussy, a gorgeous Russian Blue; Li'l Tyke, a red-flame Siamese; and Guernsey May, a cute petite black-and-white cow kitty.

Quiet observed. She thought she recognized the scent from when she first arrived, but she hadn't seen the kitties. They were in the other room. While Quiet and I ran around, Maxamussy and Guernsey May hid under the bed, and Li'l Tyke jumped on the kitchen counter. I realized it was probably the first time Quiet had been around kitties.

"No, I've been around kitties before," she told me. "I know the scent, but I can't go into that now." But she began shaking.

"What is it?" I asked her. "These are our friends. They'll warm up to you soon. You have to tell me what's wrong."

"I'll tell you later," she said. I could barely hear her. She was glancing up at the unfamiliar sounds coming from the cage overhead and glad for the distraction.

She sniffed something totally new. Two parakeets named Joey and Skye were talking. The kitties and the parakeets hadn't been formally introduced yet. The meetings happened gently and naturally.

Quiet was very relaxed around them, which was good. Wendy called us to the kitchen to serve us our dinner. I began eating but stopped to look at Quiet. Her nose twitched, and she turned away from the bowl, eyeing the kitties, as they sat across the kitchen, enjoying their dinner. She nosed their food.

I had to admit that cat food was tasty. Maxamussy ate thoughtfully, occasionally meeting Quiet's eye and checking her out. Li'l Tyke gobbled his dinner down and slowly walked toward Quiet. He sniffed her rear paws. She suddenly fell onto her back and let him have a good sniff.

Then he went for her food! He was a little piggy! Wendy escorted him from the kitchen. But Quiet didn't mind someone else drooling over her food.

Li'l Tyke was the comedian of the group and the most outgoing. He was named appropriately until the age of two, when he reached twenty pounds. Wendy nicknamed him Li'l Titanic.

Guernsey May kept to herself and didn't pay much attention to our newest member of the family. Wendy, reminded of a Jersey cow, originally named her Jersey May, but her vet told Wendy she was a Guernsey cow. Years later, we learned that was wrong, too. She was actually a Holstein, but Guernsey stuck. At least we got May right—she was born in May.

She was unique with two black markings perfectly placed on her pink nose, making it look like she had two black boogers. She was adorable.

All the kitties accepted Quiet. Who wouldn't? Quiet was very comfortable with them.

"I've only been here a few hours, but I feel a peace in this home and a lot of love," she told me.

I was almost done with my food when I saw Quiet staring at me. I took another bite and looked at her, doing my best to show her what to do, and it was OK to eat. She still refused.

Finally, Wendy sat on the floor beside Quiet, took a finger of wet food, and offered it to her. "Look. It's got carrots and peas," she said, trying to make it sound fun.

Quiet looked at Wendy as if she was nuts, then at Wendy's finger. She sniffed it and gently licked it in slow motion.

"Good, huh?" Wendy scooped another finger full.

Quiet licked from her finger again. That was how she finished her first meal with us.

🐾

Around ten o'clock that evening, we were getting concerned for Quiet. She had finished her first meal and had plenty of water, thanks to my showing her how to lap up a bowlful. She must surely need to go to the bathroom.

"Let's pay visits," I told Quiet.

Off we went. Wendy was shocked to see Quiet fly out the door with me. I wasn't. She walked alongside me except when I stopped, when she quickly ducked under me. She still didn't pee.

We turned around, and Wendy said, "Come on. You can do it. You're in America. You're free to pee anywhere and everywhere!"

Suddenly, Quiet stopped, squatted, and peed.

"Yay!" Wendy said. "You did it! You're liberated. Good girl, Liberty. Good girl, Liberty Pearl!"

From that moment on, Quiet was called Liberty Pearl.

🐾

Marcy called the next day to ask how we were doing.

"Beautiful," Wendy said. "Quiet peed. She found her freedom. She's an American. What do you think of calling her Liberty Pearl?"

"I love it. It's a dignified name for a courageous little war hero."

Liberty Pearl had found her forever home.

4

Savannah's New Mission

I loved my new little friend and took her on as my own. We were inseparable. Wendy hardly had to do anything. I was grateful that I could help out. Everything I did, Liberty Pearl copied. I went for water, and she followed. When I stopped drinking, she took over the bowl after waiting patiently.

The same thing happened when we had treats or dinner. I started eating but stopped to eye her on. We snuggled together to sleep on the floor. If I got up to change spots, within seconds, Liberty Pearl followed me and plopped back down against my stomach and chest. I constantly licked her, especially her face, trying to wipe away all her tears and comfort her as much as I could.

With Wendy, Liberty Pearl seemed eager to please, though there were times when intense fear overcame her and made her confused and flustered. She wanted to let me into her experiences. She started to tell me many times but stopped and stared into space, shaking uncontrollably.

I knew it would take time, and I would give her all the space she needed. She would tell me when she was ready. I couldn't begin to imagine what that little dog had been through. What was her life like before the bombings? Where did she come from?

Wendy let me take the reins. I was with Liberty Pearl every second, calming her with every step, showing her what to do. In our dog language, I communicated to Liberty Pearl exactly what was happening and how to behave.

Wendy thought it was a miracle to watch our relationship unfold and how Liberty Pearl quickly adapted through the process. I thought it was just nature doing its thing.

Slowly, Liberty Pearl began doing her bathroom business but still scantily and carefully, which meant we needed more-frequent walks. For Wendy and me, it didn't matter how long it took or how difficult it was. We were there for Liberty Pearl no matter what. We would do anything for that little angel. Encouragement and love were our mantra from day one.

Liberty Pearl didn't have a nasty bone in her body. She never grumbled or complained. Sometimes, we wished she would.

"Tell me what you're feeling, Liberty Pearl," Wendy said. "How can I do better?"

Liberty Pearl's stare could tell a thousand stories. Her

walleye made her storytelling urgent and even more precious. Wendy and I prayed for the day it would be a happy story. On rare occasions, we glimpsed joyful moments coming from her.

Wendy made a little game of blowing a raspberry on her tummy when she lay on her back. She did that and then got nose-to-nose with Liberty Pearl and looked her in the eye, saying "Oh," very slowly, repeating the word several times. Then she blew another raspberry and said "Oh" again.

Liberty Pearl finally gave a playful sneeze and put her mouth to Wendy's. After a few of those raspberry moments, she met Wendy's mouth with a little lick. We had a major breakthrough. She was beginning to have fun and relax a little. We began calling her "Libby" after a few weeks, and she seemed to like it.

At bedtime, Wendy had a tradition of hiding doggie cookies under her pillow. She'd pretend not to know the cookies were there while she brushed her teeth and got ready for bed. Every night I fell for it, excited to have my treat. Then when Wendy got into bed, she'd ask me, "What is it? You're moving the pillow...oh is something there?" She'd lift the pillow and exclaim, "Why the cookie fairy was here." Liberty Pearl loved the ritual and gobbled up her treats quicker than I did.

5
The Beginnings in Iraq

Two weeks after Liberty Pearl moved in, while we were taking our afternoon snooze, a helicopter flew over the house. The sound grew intense, as the pilot must have been searching for somebody right in our neighborhood.

Liberty Pearl began convulsing from head to toe. Her body was like a little machine gun, unable to shut itself off.

"Bombs!" she told me. "We're going to be hit!"

I assured her there were no bombs and placed a paw on top of her. I licked her face as lovingly as I could. Try as I might, she kept shaking. My heart sank. She had to start telling me about her life soon, because she needed to get her fears off her chest.

As quickly as the helicopter appeared, it left, but Liberty Pearl still shook.

Suddenly, she started telling me her story.

"I think I came from a Paris breeder. I had to have

come from somewhere outside the country. There are no small dogs in Iraq. I was the only one."

I was surprised by the outburst, but glad she was finally opening up.

"After my rescue from under the dusty rubble in the Palace, a long, tedious plan was created to keep me safe."

There was no way I could come close to explaining the actual experience of her rescue. I'm retelling it as best I can. Libby spoke in broken sentences. It seemed difficult for her to even state the facts. It was too painful, and her memory was hazy at times.

🐾

Marcy told us that all who were involved in rescuing Liberty Pearl were working independently. International rescues weren't the norm. In the Middle East, there was little precedent to care for a dog, let alone rescue one. There were no dogs or cats until the 1800s, when the English settled in Iraq and brought their dogs, mainly New Canaan Hounds. That started the dog population, and all the dogs were medium to large. There were no pure breeds. The brutal truth is that dogs in that part of the world are mainly strays that live in garbage dumps and have to fend for themselves to find whatever food they can. They're often poisoned on the streets, used for target practice, or fed to lions in the zoo. Who would rescue such critters? There was a war going on.

Marcy told us the details of Liberty Pearl's rescue.

Soldiers began befriending strays, often taking care of them. In April, 2003, there was a TV report about a unit of soldiers who found four puppies stranded in the desert near the Jordan and Iraq border. Marcy watched the report in terror, as the puppies ran around several bombed-out tanks. She'd been deeply involved in dog rescues for years, and she immediately began her mission to do something for those stranded pups.

She knew a few British animal-rescue ladies and contacted them. One was Margaret Ledger. With her husband, Peter, she founded the Humane Center for Animal Welfare in Amman, Jordan. Accompanied by two military officers, Margaret gathered up the four puppies. They also found the puppies' mother in a ditch, totally debilitated but alive.

Without any resources other than keeping the dogs protected for the time being, Marcy and Margaret miraculously arranged for the dogs to be flown from Jordan to LAX via Air France Cargo. The happy news was that the mama dog is still alive and living in Encino, California. Unfortunately, one of the puppies living with her, named Jessica, died in the spring of 2016. The second puppy died early on, while the other two went to Virginia. One of the puppies, the runt of the litter, is still alive. That was the grassroots beginnings of future international dog rescues, including Liberty Pearl.

Marcy told us that soon after Mom and her pups escaped, two soldiers mentioned another rescue to an Iraqi trainee stationed at the Baghdad Zoo. The trainee contacted Marcy and told her three dogs had been brought to the zoo, with many more arriving. The military men felt sorry for them and wanted to protect them. She hoped Marcy could save the dogs.

She did, but it took months. They had to wait until it was safe to move them. There were no commercial flights in or out of Baghdad, so the dogs had to go through Jordan, and there were no resources for such a thing. No one had cages for transport, let along collars, leashes, or dog food.

Marcy sent twenty cages by DHL to the zoo. That would ensure some dogs' safe transport when the time came. Amazingly, all were spoken for and went to homes, mainly to soldiers who befriended them. There were still several dogs without homes.

One was a little white puppy that came out from under the debris of Saddam Hussein's Presidential Palace. No one was sure if the little dog would survive.

"You suffered a concussion and were in shock," Marcy reminded Liberty Pearl.

Dogs were rescued from two of the palaces. A military person adopted Saddam's son's German Shepherd. Through Marcy's program, he took the Shepherd home with him to Tennessee. He wanted the dog intact but Marcy was adamant about having the dog neutered before he left. She sensed he was going to breed the dog. She saw dollar signs in the soldier's eyes as the pups would be known as Hussein's son's dogs.

Marcy immediately made arrangements for the little white puppy to be rescued if she survived.

In the meantime, the Baghdad Zoo seemed the safest and most-feasible place for the dogs. The zoo had been bombed, killing many animals, which meant some empty cages. Another young woman, Colonel Susan played a big role in caring for the little white puppy and the rest of the orphaned animals. Liberty Pearl was friends with Lucky, a dog Colonel Susan adopted. Liberty Pearl and Lucky would later make their escape to the States together. Liberty Pearl and her cellmate, the pelican, would be "roommates" for eight months.

"You were originally named Pelican 2," Marcy reminded Liberty Pearl.

Beside them in another cage was a dog rooming with a bear. Somehow, it all worked. Pelican 2 never made a sound.

"My fear was too great," Liberty Pearl explained. "I liked the other dogs, but I was beyond shell-shocked."

Meanwhile, the other dogs always made a racket when someone came around. Liberty Pearl was so terrified, she always rolled onto her back with her legs in the air, waiting for death.

Everyone was concerned about her. She barely ate, and she was always lethargic. Colonel Susan thought she might be a Maltese, which was the right size. It wasn't until eighteen months later that we learned she was a purebred Coton de Tulear, a breed from Madagascar, so it made sense that she came from Paris.

"I was about three months old when I was rescued," Liberty Pearl said.

She didn't grow. At six months, she was about the same size as when she was rescued. Female Cotons usually reach twelve to fifteen pounds, but she weighed only five.

"Maybe it was better they didn't know my true heritage," Liberty Pearl added.

Colonel Susan brought special treats when she could. That meant part of her lunch or dinner.

"There was no dog food in Iraq," Marcy said. "It wasn't allowed even if they could supply it, because it might contain pork, and that's not allowed in Iraq."

The dogs ate mainly bread and rice. They never got dog food. Many of the soldiers who befriended the stray dogs in Iraq shared their MREs, Meals Ready to Eat, with their new friends. Often, those dogs became loyal companions to the soldiers and often saved their lives.

Marcy told us of one very sad story; A soldier had contacted Marcy to arrange for her dog to be sent home to her once she was finished with combat. She was killed when she had only two weeks left. Her parents contacted Marcy and asked her to please send their daughter's dog to them. At least the soldier got her wish for her dear companion.

The best news was that soldiers who befriended a dog could have the dog sent home. It became part of the Iraqi dog movement, one of the good things that came out of Iraq.

6

Escape from Iraq

66 I remained in the zoo for eight months before my dangerous journey over the border to Amman, Jordan," Liberty Pearl continued. "I was one of the first dogs in a truckload to escape. During my time at the zoo, I endured horrendous trials of my will. The beautiful souls of the few cats they found, along with many stray dogs, were fed to the lions. Those polarizing screams filled the hot Iraqi air. I thought my life was over."

She began shaking. "I'll never get over it."

My fur rose just thinking about it.

✿

One day I woke with Liberty Pearl frantically licking my ear. She had just had a bad dream.

"I might be next!" she said. "Help me!"

"It was just a dream," I assured her, shuddering along with her, though I tried to hide it by standing over her and cleaning her belly to calm her.

Whimpering, Liberty Pearl added "It could have been me. It could have been me."

I wondered what thoughts the surviving dogs had. They were safe in their cells, surrounded by murderers. Or were they safe? What if one of them was next? Such fear lived in every muscle.

Again, Liberty Pearl told us about how she would sit under the leaky faucet to cool her head from the day's heat and to escape the reality of things happening around her.

She was very smart, but nothing could help her escape the horrible stench and the chill of many innocent cats and dogs being sacrificed. She shook constantly during those rituals.

Pelican was a great comfort for her. I asked her what it was like living with a pelican.

"Pelican often lay down beside me," Liberty Pearl said. We shared the small puddle from the leaky faucet. Who knows where Pelican came from? Pelicans can either be ocean or lake birds. He never told me. He was very young when he came to live in the zoo. Whatever water he came from, he seemed content and liked me."

Liberty Pearl continued. "Months passed. The desert heat made it seem like time stood still. I was lethargic, though I ate as much as I could. I warmed up to Colonel Susan, giving her soft, wet kisses and snuggles that lasted fifteen seconds. I trusted her touch."

"When a man appeared, I started shaking and tried to burrow into the cement. At the palace, handlers took care

of our feedings and bathroom duties. They wore intimidating gloves."

In Iraq and many of the Middle Eastern countries, a
person who handles an animal must bathe seven times
before they can pray. Dogs and cats weren't respected
by many. Some were used for target practice. If anyone
owned a dog, it was always for protection, and the dog
lived outside. In Jordan, dogs owned by Christian Arabs
live on their owners' roofs.

It was clear to me that the handlers were not compas-
sionate with any of the animals they cared for. However,
Hussein's daughters must have loved, touched, and cuddled their pup. That was probably why Liberty Pearl was
comfortable with women.

"The day finally came for our long trip to Jordan," she
said. "It was a tedious ten-hour drive through Iraq and
Jordan's terrible terrain, with frequent stops by the military. It took us six hours to reach the Jordanian border,
then four more to arrive at the Humane Center for Animal
Welfare in Amman. Marcy arranged for Lucky to leave
with me as a surprise for Colonel Susan, because she had
leave to go to California. We were in a truck with twelve
other dogs."

It was a risky trip. Many soldiers tried to take their
loyal, adopted buddies with them. On a very rare occa-
sion an untrained dog would instinctively sniff out a hidden mine placed randomly in the region and saved many
lives. Those dogs slept, ate, and fought with their new

guardians. When it was time for the soldier to relocate or go back to the States, they wanted their best friend to come with them. Many tried to sneak their buddies out. Unfortunately, if they were stopped at an inspection, many of those dogs were shot and killed, because the unit couldn't afford a barking dog that might give them away in enemy territory. They had to remain unseen and unheard.

I thought that would be easy for Liberty Pearl.

"Because we had to remain hidden, there were no pee breaks. If we were let out, besides the risk of being caught, we might step on a mine or run away. We had to stay in the truck for the whole ten hours.

The trip was in our favor. We sneaked over Jordan's border without any mishap or delay. Margaret Ledger anxiously awaited our arrival at the Humane Center for Animal Welfare. She gave me as much love as she could, but after a few seconds, I bolted under her couch in case there was a bomb.

Lucky and I were taken to the animal facility, where we were given a thorough medical exam before our long, tedious flight to the U.S. Marcy was adamant that we be spayed and neutered. It turned out I was too weak for surgery, so that had to wait until I was in the States, but Lucky was neutered.

The Human Society for Animal Welfare had to hire a British vet to do the procedures, because none of the Iraqi vets knew how. It took Lucky a few days to recoup. Finally, we were placed in a large crate, boarded Air France

Cargo, and started our 18 hours 19 minutes flight to LAX with one two-hour stopover in Paris. Altogether, fourteen dogs boarded that plane in December, 2003. Our rescue was successful, thank goodness. But once we landed, as we left the plane, all these people were taking photos of us. It was late at night so there was a mean downpour of flashing lights from the cameras that scared me to death. I was clearly in a panic mode."

"The worst is over," I kept telling Liberty Pearl. She knew I was right, but it would take time for her to really understand that she finally had all the time and freedom she needed.

7

A Close Call

We had one major scare in the first weeks that Liberty Pearl who we now called "Libby" lived with us. We were taking her for a walk in Gini's neighborhood, and Wendy somehow lost Libby's leash. It slipped through her fingers and lay on the pavement. Wendy stomped her foot on it, but her sandal made a loud *smack* when it hit the concrete, and it startled me and scared the heck out of Libby. She bolted down the street so fast, there was no way to fetch her. I would have, but I felt I needed to stay by Wendy's side, because I trusted her to do the right thing.

She held onto me and took Gini and me to the car to drive down the streets.

"Oh, my God, what have I done? This little angel travels around the globe to sunny California, and I lose her within a month!" Wendy said. "Please, God, don't let her be hit. She's so terrified, she's out of control. She might run anywhere."

Our search began. We saw a lady and her daughter and asked if they saw a little white dog with a red leash, and they pointed to where Libby ran up another street. Rather than chase her, we drove around the block to come from the other direction to meet her.

We ended back where we began, with the woman and her daughter, and sure enough, we saw another woman who had Libby!

Wendy had tears streaming down her cheeks, saying "Oh, thank you! Thank you!"

"Is this your dog?" the woman asked.

Couldn't she tell? Wendy was a mess.

"Yes, she's my dog. Her name is Liberty Pearl. Look at the tag."

The woman checked, and I was glad she was being careful, then she handed Libby to us.

We were very lucky. We certainly had a guardian angel with us that day. Such a thing never happened again. Wendy's hand was glued to that leash. I promised myself I'd run after Libby if she ever did that again.

✥

Libby was finding herself in her own time. One night, she surprised us by trying my special meal. Wendy has pasta for most dinners. She makes it with olive oil and garlic, rotating broccoli or zucchini. Every night, she gave me my regular food, but I never ate it right off. I waited, anticipating the sound of her taking out the big pot and filling it with water.

When I heard it, I knew it was pasta time. Then I sat

near my other empty bowl and savored the moment when she dished out my portion. I ate it fast. After I cleaned the bowl, I ate my dinner.

That went on for years. Wendy and I often wondered if that combination of olive oil, garlic, and veggies extended my life. I like to think that.

"I watched Savannah inhale it," Libby said, "and I was curious. Wendy dished out a sample for me. I ate the broccoli but left the pasta. After a few more servings, I began eating the pasta, too. I needed to put on weight, and that did the trick."

Wendy spent a lot of time with her mom, Gini, and her dad, Alan, who Wendy called "Angus," which was his real name, as they grew older and needed special care. They lived only five minutes away. Though they were divorced, they lived in the same condo complex across the hall from each other, which made it very easy. It was nice that Gini and Angus got along great. I loved getting into the car each day and driving to their homes. It was a treat.

Angus had two kitties named Mac and Tosh. We rescued them from a horrible situation. They were tiny kittens named Hops and Barley when we first met them in front of their house. The owners were known drug addicts. Their last kitty died of a drug overdose. Apparently, someone thought it was funny to give drugs to a beautiful Persian cat named Catzilla. We wouldn't allow those two kittens to be exposed to such a life.

One day, Mac came up to me and licked me, then followed us home. That was an easy rescue, but it took months before we could carefully abduct his brother. When we did, Angus became infatuated with the two cats. I loved them, too, though Tosh wasn't very friendly.

Angus adored me and called me, "The best dog ever in my lifetime." And he fell in love with Libby. Who wouldn't?

He used to kid us and said, "Watch it, Dear. Libby might be hiding a missile."

He was a comedian and could get away with saying things like that. He loved watching our antics and how Libby tucked herself neatly against my tummy.

"This is pure unconditional love at its zenith," Angus said. "If only all of us could be like that." He looked at me and continued, "Watching the day to day loving relation-ship between you, with your motherly doting, and dear little traumatized Libby is the most healing, fascinating joy I've ever experienced."

Sometimes when Libby would lie with me, Angus and Wendy would tease her by saying "Hi" several times. When that happened, Libby would raise one back leg straight up. They would say, "Look, Libby's raising the American flag." Also, Angus and Wendy gave Libby the nickname of "Snow Shoes." She had hairy paws which made her feet look bigger than they are. They said she looked ready for the ski slopes. She just needed her skis.

The first few months Libby lived with us, we had to stage a little game. We lived in an old apartment complex and discovered mold on the windowsills. Wendy told the manager and the landlord, but they didn't do anything. She called Building and Safety, and that person said we had mold in our walls.

The owners weren't happy with Wendy after that and harassed her over every little thing. Dogs were no longer allowed to live on the premises. I was grandfathered into the lease, though, so I was OK. Liberty Pearl was another matter. We came up with a plan as we began looking for another place to live.

Carlos was a dear friend of ours who stayed in our house to care for all of us whenever Wendy had to leave town. He came over frequently for dinner and hung out with us for our midnight walks.

Wendy had a white rhinoceros stuffed toy that was Libby's size, though she was finally starting to fill out. We had an extra red collar and matching leash. Wendy placed the collar and leash on the stuffed white rhino and gave it to Carlos to carry under his arm whenever he left, so any spy might see it. They'd think it was Libby. He always brought it with him when he arrived, too.

"When we went for our walks Carlos carried me down the steps and through the complex just like he would with the rhino. We had our walks, and Carlos carried me back in his arms," Libby said.

It worked great. We never had a phone call or written notice about the extra dog. We got away with it for two full months. It was a good thing we moved, though, because Libby was finally gaining weight. When she arrived from Marcy, she was seven pounds, but within four months, she gained five pounds.

8

The Move with Marmaladee's Arrival

On August 27, 2004, we moved from the apartment to a cute little townhouse in Toluca Lake. All of us critters took the move very well. Excited to sniff our new domain, Libby and I couldn't wait to walk the neighborhood. There were so many new smells, sounds, and people walking their dogs. Wendy's family came to the new home for Thanksgiving. Christmas came and went. We were happily settled into our new surroundings and loved our new neighbors.

In January, Libby and I went with Wendy on our usual visit to one of our favorite pet stores, Petmania in Burbank. Our other favorite store was Rusty's in Studio City. Petmania rescued dogs, cats, rabbits, birds, and anything else they could. We loved meeting the newcomers. I especially had to introduce myself to every homeless kitty in the place.

I had a secret plan that Libby would befriend the first kitty I saw. That Sunday, there was only one little kitten alone in a large cage. Wendy and I went to say hello to the beautiful golden-red tabby. She was a girl, which was rare for that coloring.

I gave her one sniff, then, much to Wendy and my own amazement, I walked past her to meet a rabbit. I wanted Libby to have the opportunity to be introduced to a new kitty, but she was too scared. She shook like mad. She still suffered from PTSD whenever we left the house, except at Wendy's parents' place. Even during our walks, depending on who was coming toward us, her radar was extremely keen.

On a recent walk Libby began trembling in complete terror, she couldn't control it and hid under me, making all of us stop. She was in a frenzy.

Wendy and I tried to calm Libby to no avail. A moment later, a dark-skinned man came around the corner and walked toward us. He looked Middle Eastern. His scent struck a sensitive nerve in her memories that hit her like a twenty-foot tidal wave.

We managed to cross the street, so the innocent man could continue down the sidewalk. Wendy sat beside Libby, trying to comfort her as best she could.

I stood over Libby like a statue guarding its post. The unknowing man passed us and waved. We must have looked a sight, all of us clumped over a little white mass of nerves.

Wendy waved back and said, "It's a friend, Libby, a friend."

She said that every time we met a stranger, hoping to ease Libby's fear. It eventually began to work, but not that day.

"I was too nervous," Libby said. "I couldn't stop shaking. I was afraid the man would take me away. He smelled like the handler that took me outside to 'pay visits.' I finally settled down in a few minutes to continue our walk."

The pet shop had a front door, and Libby was on a mission to get out that door as fast as she could. Wendy consoled her and said, "Baby-girl be brave."

Even my presence didn't help. I was busy sniffing the rabbit. Wendy turned to fetch me and pay for our things. We were about to leave when the store owner said, "I think you need to take that little kitten home."

Wendy looked at her in confusion.

The owner pointed at the cage. "Look."

The kitten had its paw out of the cage and was petting Libby's back, stroking her and purring.

Wendy was shocked, but I knew immediately and went to Libby to say, "There you go, Libby. You have your first conquest."

"I liked the kitten's affection," Libby said, but I still wanted to get out of the store."

We went to the register to pay for our food.

"So, are you taking her?" the owner asked.

"I've already got three kitties, two birds, and two dogs. I don't think I can handle any more," Wendy said.

We left.

✿

Later that night, Wendy was thinking of names for the kitten. She tried, "Lady Cassandra, Cassie, Chloe, Lady Marmalade, Marmaladee. Hmmm."

The next day, we went to bring Marmaladee home.

"What's another kitty?" I wondered.

The new kitten scampered around her new home for hours. A dear friend of Wendy's, Jayne, came over for dinner that evening, and we became concerned for Marmaladee. She didn't stop jumping around, from the couch to the stairs to the piano to the TV shelf.

Jayne forced a time out and scooped her into her arms. "Her heart's racing," she said.

Marmaladee exhausted, fell asleep within seconds.

"When she woke she walked right up to me to sniff," Libby said. "I nudged and kissed her, really liking her. She was my first kitty. It felt comforting. Then she snuggled up between me and Li'l Tyke. He welcomed her and began to clean her."

It seemed that Marmaladee was home.

9
Gracefully Landing

Within a couple more months, Libby had gained two more pounds, making her weight fourteen pounds. It was perfect. She felt well, and her coat blossomed into a full-body perm of long, soft, flowing hair.

We were walking one day when a passerby remarked how adorable Libby and I were walking side-by-side and how cute it was that Libby hid under me.

"Oh, you have a Coton de Tulear," the woman said.

"A who? A what?" Wendy asked.

"A Coton de Tulear. She's lovely."

When we got home, Wendy immediately went online and looked it up. Sure enough, on the Coton de Tulear website we stared at a very similar face and body. The dog had the same coloring, white with a bit of gold markings on her ears. Libby had what they called a "cigar-colored nose," pink with a slightly darker rim. Wendy knew all along that Libby wasn't a Maltese, but she couldn't figure out what she could be.

We finally knew she was a Coton de Tulear. Wendy

brushed her every day and told her what a beautiful girl she was. Her hair blew in the breeze. Wendy took her to a groomer once, and, when we picked her up, Wendy couldn't stop laughing. The groomers blow-dried Libby's hair, and it stood up all over her body. She looked like she had stuck her paw into a light fixture.

She was beautiful. Even with her concussion and her walleye, she looked royal. After all, she once belonged to King Hussein, making her a princess.

In late December, 2005, we fostered and ended up keeping Elmo, a diabetic kitty. His owners couldn't deal with it and took him to a vet to be put down. That was horrible. An assistant to the vet knew about Wendy and asked if she would be willing to save this little—well, large—fella.

He soon became our Mr. Soul Man. Elmo was scared and grumpy when Wendy first brought him into our fold. We smelled the fear and left him alone. Wendy sang to him *Mr. Soul Man* from the Blues Brothers. She didn't know all the words, so she replaced the lyrics with the words "boom booms." This became a nightly occurrence before lights went out.

Wendy serenaded him, and he soon joined in with a cheerful "mew" that was perfectly timed between the "boom booms." He became a very happy boy and a permanent member of our family.

Maxamussy's nose was out of joint. He didn't care for Elmo. Fur flew every day. Elmo had to go to the vet and be put on antibiotics after a bad scratch from Maxamussy. He had to be shaved, and it looked like Maxamussy drew a perfect Z for Zorro down his back. They managed a truce after that. One of them won the dominance deal.

So, I had another crush, and I washed Elmo's ears, mouth, and eyes. Libby was getting more and more outgoing with her love and affection. She was still shy with people, especially men, but she was blossoming. She was calmer and more engaged. Libby's role of motherly dominance slowly took over. She pampered me, checking me constantly, as I rested more those days. Our roles began to reverse.

As time continued, I taught Libby more about life. She loved it and became quite a character. She displayed more joy each day and had boundless love for me, Wendy, and the kitties. She still shook when she went to a new place or met new people, but it wasn't as frantic. Hiding under me was still her safe haven. She loved car rides and anything where I was involved.

I'd been going with Wendy to her performing arts classes for special-needs people for years, so it was natural for Libby to join us.

"At first, it was a little overwhelming," Libby told me. "There were so many people in one room! I was still lying on my back and doing the step-on-me-and-get-it-over-with routine. The kids, seeing I was frightened, offered me calm, love, and personal space. Soon, I came out from under Savannah and sniffed one or two of the students. My curiosity forced me to make more of an appearance. Whenever I felt uncomfortable, I jumped for cover under Savannah."

As scared as Libby was, she was also bold. We saw her trying harder all the time.

10

Growing Pains

2006 started off with a lot of sadness. The first week of January, Joey, our green parakeet, passed away. Skye followed a year and a half later. Then on January 29, our beautiful Maxamussy passed on.

My heart ached for quite awhile after we lost Maxamussy. When "Max" was a little kitten, I carried him around in my mouth. He was rescued all by himself near a railroad track in the San Fernando Valley. We slept together constantly. He was mine.

Guernsey May had loved Max and had followed him everywhere. When he died she slowly came up to him, sniffed him and quickly ran away. Libby and I hovered over his body, sniffing and nudging to say our good-byes.

"I caught a familiar scent," Libby said. It was death, and it scared me. All I could think of was the smell in the air at the zoo, where so many cats were killed by lions. I hid under Savannah."

Wendy thought we were trying to get Max to wake up, or maybe she just wished we were. It was a strange evening.

An hour before Max passed on, a neighborhood feral kitty we befriended jumped into our patio, ran around, and jumped out. He and Max had been sorting out their territory. He'd been coming around more frequently.

It started one night while Wendy was calling all the critters inside from the patio, and she saw Guernsey May peering at her from a tree.

"Guernsey May, come down and come inside."

Wendy went into the kitchen and saw Guernsey May at her food dish. She went back outside and saw another cow kitty peeking at us.

"Holy cow, no pun intended, but you look just like Guernsey May," Wendy said.

Seeing it was a male cat, she named him Guernsey Bob. He started following us on our walks. It was ironic that Guernsey May and Wendy also met from her peering from up in a tree.

In August 2001, Wendy went to the East Valley shelter to adopt a kitty for a friend. The friend couldn't bear the thought of going to the shelter, so she asked Wendy to go for her. Wendy heard they had a Siamese up for adoption.

As she walked from the parking lot to the front door of the shelter, she heard a cat mewing. She stopped, and the front door opened, and someone came out. The person passed Wendy, and she walked toward the front door again. Intense mewing came again.

Wendy saw a little boy standing there with a crate. "Do you have a little kitty in there?"

He shook his head "no."

Again, the front door opened, and a family left. The kitten was silent.

Finally, Wendy was almost at the door, and the kitten mewed again. Wendy turned and looked up at a tree. An adorable face stared down at her. It was a black-and-white kitten, maybe three months old, with a pink nose and two perfectly drawn black boogers around each nostril.

"Mew!" she said again.

Wendy held out her arms, and the frightened kitten immediately ran down to her. The front door opened behind Wendy, and the kitten scampered back up the tree in fright.

Wendy went to her car, where she always kept a supply of dog and cat kibble for just such situations. She offered the kitten food from her hand, and it returned. She put her in the cat carrier meant for the Siamese and quickly walked into the shelter to ask if the Siamese was available, but she'd been adopted.

Wendy took the little kitten to her car and introduced her to her friend, Meryl, who wanted the Siamese. Meryl fell in love with the kitten and kept her for a few days, but her allergies were so bad, she had to return it to Wendy.

Wendy had to keep her. She was so precious. She wondered where the kitten came from. Was she feral, or had someone dropped her off in a box at the shelter? People did that without thinking of the consequences.

The kitten was a bit skittish but soon warmed up to

the other kitties. At that time, Charee, a lovely charcoal-colored part-Persian girl was with us along with Li'l Tyke, and Maxamussy. They all hit it off famously. Charee became the mom to Guernsey May.

The night we lost Maxamussy, Wendy leashed us up to go for our walks around eleven o'clock, then a report came that *World News Tonight* anchor Bob Woodruff and cameraman Doug Vogt had been seriously injured in Iraq. We sat and listened to the report for twenty minutes. This news interrupted our sadness of Maxamussy's passing.

Still, we were heartbroken, and Guernsey May and Wendy took it hard. Guernsey May didn't come down from upstairs for six months except to eat. The minute she finished, she scurried up the stairs. Li'l Tyke, Max's litter mate, seemed to take his passing OK, and so did Marmaladee.

11

Cheweybacca

In April, 2007, Wendy rescued a little Terrier mix and his brother from the East Valley Shelter where I'd once been. Wendy named the Terrier "Cheweybacca," because he resembled the *Star Wars* character "Chewbacca." His brother was named Pepper, which Wendy quickly changed to Sergeant Pepper, because that little dog was a terror! We found him a home within a few days. "Chewey" was a sweet, loving little dog and showed plenty of love to our female friends, especially Michelle and her dog, Nikko. Michelle quickly nicknamed him Romeo.

He soon turned into Cujo. His alter ego was terrified of men, especially Hispanics. He came from a Hispanic step-dad who believed in physical punishment. Chewey became quite agitated. Wendy had to watch him, as he would lash out, showing teeth to any unsuspecting male who dared pass us on the street. He was more difficult to adopt out. Although she put him up for adoption, Wendy was falling in love with him, and she got a pang in her gut when someone showed any interest in him. Wendy was hooked.

Libby chimed in, "We didn't need another dog, but I loved Chewey. We were the same size and became instant friends. We had great play times together. He became submissive and allowed me to dominate him, which made me feel good and gave me more confidence."

Chewey loved to lick. He had the longest tongue in the west. Wendy constantly told him to stop licking. Unfortunately, he also had a Napoleon complex. He began attacking me. I placed my paw on Chewey to stop him, which worked in the beginning, but the situation gradually became serious.

One day, he attacked me in the car. Blood was drawn from Wendy's hand when she tried to stop the battle. I had already earned my peace at the age of fifteen. Gini's dog Beau just passed, and Gini was lonely. She told Wendy she wanted Chewey, so he moved in with her. It worked out for the best after all.

During our visits with Gini and Chewey, Libby and Chewey made up for lost time, romping, play-fighting, and kissing like crazy. Libby made funny little noises in her glee, almost like she was saying, "Ollie-up!"

I watched patiently, content with my thoughts, but I still kept my guard up. Chewey was always unpredictable. I loved the little guy, but he was a bit nuts. He appeared to still have respect for me. I just wished he didn't think of me as intimidating. I would rather be a friend. He refused to get over his Napoleon complex.

After Chewey moved in with Gini, Wendy enrolled him

in agility classes. He went through dog training, but he needed more exposure to other dogs and people. The classes were perfect.

"I went through dog training, too," Libby said. "Of course, I soon became the princess of the class. I wanted nothing to do with it and felt it was beneath me. I drearily went through the motions."

If a dog could show boredom, Libby deserved a blue ribbon. Those classes weren't for her. I used to go and watch.

"Sit," Wendy said.

"What?" Libby asked. "I won't dirty my bum on a cement ground."

"Lie down."

Libby looked at her like she was crazy. "Why?"

I don't remember how, but Libby was awarded a certificate of completion for the course.

Chewey was great in the agility classes. He seemed to enjoy himself. The trainer placed Chewey with a male handler, while Wendy took his dog, so Chewey could raise his confidence with a male. That really worked.

Libby sat with me to watch Chewey. I enjoyed what they did and wondered why Wendy never had me take an agility course. I would have aced it. Wendy looked at me, and I saw that she agreed.

"I wish we'd done this, Savannah," Wendy said. "If I had only discovered this when you were younger."

I knew in my heart of hearts that when I was a young

dog, had we been exposed to agility training, I would have been the best. I was a fast runner. Wendy threw tennis balls for me for ten years, and I wouldn't let her stop. She had a strong arm. Once while we played, some baseball players watched her throw the ball. I caught it and brought it back to her. One of the guys asked if I could be on their team.

"She only works union," Wendy said.

She was being a smart aleck.

12

Liberty Pearl Finds Herself

Libby grew significantly and became a little comedienne. She was more confident, too. One evening while watching the news, there was a report that Saddam Hussein had been captured and was about to be hanged. Mosque music played in the background.

Suddenly, we heard growling, which was very rare. I didn't growl hardly ever, and Libby didn't even speak that language, or so I thought.

Wendy looked around to see if someone was loitering outside the front door, but there was no one. The growling began again, and she looked at me, lying at her feet. We looked at Libby and saw her on the ground, her front legs stretched out ahead of her, her mouth slightly open, growling. The music from the TV made her squirm.

"I don't like how it made me feel! The voices took me back to a place I didn't want to be. It was a new sensation to growl. I don't know where it came from, but it felt good."

Wendy, shocked, wished she had videotaped it. No one would believe her story. It was clear Libby still carried memories and fear in her bones. We were glad she spoke up.

"Good girl," Wendy said. "You tell 'em." She told me she never liked the Mosque sounds. Now that she lives in Los Angeles, she loves listening to The Eagles, the California-based band. "This is much more my style," she told me.

I was slowing down. I enjoyed my several walks each day and visits to the park, but I was tired after fetching the ball just a few times. I also had the early stages of incontinence. When it first happened, I took Wendy to a spot where it was wet to show her. I was embarrassed. Wendy put me on Proin, a natural, chewable tablet, which helped. She also placed a tarp on the floor with a towel over it in case of an accident.

I hated it. The tarp made me hot, so Wendy got rid of it. Also, I still had some dignity left. I was doing fine on the Proin, and the towel would soak up any accident. Heck, I was sixteen by then.

One late spring evening, we took our usual midnight walk and turned right off our driveway instead of left. Upon our return, there were sprinklers on, making little puddles on the lawn beside the road. Libby stopped by a tree where the sprinklers were dying down.

I sniffed a bush just ahead of Wendy and Libby. Intrigued, I stopped suddenly, and Wendy waited. I was very intent. Then I noticed Libby was still focused on that tree. It was hard getting Libby's attention. I knew what was going on.

"Come on, Libby," Wendy said.

She finally jumped back onto the sidewalk, and we joined her. Suddenly, Wendy looked down and saw twigs hanging from Libby's mouth. What had she found near the tree that would make her eat twigs? Wendy knelt to take the twigs away and suddenly realized that the twigs had feet attached to the ends!

"Drop it," Wendy commanded.

"I did it very gently, feeling very protective," Libby said.

"Good Libby. Good job." Wendy had a tiny fledgling in her hand, with hardly any feathers. The bird was wet from the sprinklers.

Wendy immediately cupped it in her hand and breathed on the tiny body to give it warmth. She feared it was dying. How could such a frail little thing live through that?

It had obviously fallen from a nest, but how long had it been lying there?

"Good girl," Wendy told Libby. "You did a wonderful thing."

When we got home, Wendy took a bird cage she kept in storage for emergencies and placed a towel in it with a torn-up paper towel shaped into a small hill for the fledgling. The little guy was dry and had begun moving, as if waking from a dizzy stupor.

Wendy was amazed. She filled an eyedropper with warm vegetable broth and squirted some gently into its mouth. It seemed to like it.

"Libby, you rescued this little dove. He's alive because of you. Right, Savannah?"

Libby wagged her tail and looked up at Wendy, then she nudged me and kissed me.

"Savannah," Wendy told me, "you taught her well."

In 1998, I rescued a fledgling mockingbird during our midnight walk. As we went up the street, a cat from across the street followed us. She never showed herself and always ran away when we approached. She seemed terrified of me. I wanted nothing more than to meet her face-to-face, but Wendy always told me to sit to avoid scaring the kitty named "Decibel."

We continued walking, and Decibel crossed the street toward us, giving a loud meow that made us stop. She turned and walked back where she came from, then stopped and looked back at us, giving another meow.

Something was going on. She wanted us to listen and follow, so we did. When we stepped onto the sidewalk, I couldn't help myself and beelined toward the neighbor's bush on high alert, nose down for scent. Wendy walked past me and the bush. Suddenly, a tiny bird ran from the bush to the grass.

Decibel froze in her tracks, but I followed the baby bird.

Wendy, fearing the cat might pounce, followed right behind. She caught up to me and the fledgling and picked him up.

"Hey, Li'l Bubba, what are you doing out here on your own?" she asked, feeling his little heart beating against her palm, as she held him against her chest.

The little guy looked like a wild Albert Einstein, barely showing any feathers except a few attempts at sprouting them from his head. Wendy thanked the kitty for saving the little bird's life and brought him home with us.

She set him up in a cat carrier in our bathroom to provide extra security from the three kitties sitting outside the door, drooling.

Early the next morning, the bird's parents and a chorus of their friends woke us up. I had the feeling they were telling us off. Wendy went to the bathroom to check on Bubba to see him standing up, chirping at the open window toward his family.

Wendy took the carrier out to the balcony, so Mom and Dad could see their little one. From that day on for six weeks, we shared feeding privileges. The old adage "If you touch a baby bird, the parents will have nothing to do with it," turned out to be wrong. Wendy even gave Bubba flying lessons.

The only negative thing was, Bubba imprinted on Wendy, not his parents. When it was time for him to take flight, he flew away and kept returning. Wendy's dad, Angus, who cared for Bubba when Wendy was out of town, became the bird's daddy. Totally, smitten, Angus wanted to keep him. We thought about that a long time but decided it would be unfair for a wild bird to be kept captive, not to mention possibly dangerous.

Bubba sat on Wendy and Angus' shoulders and wanted to be with us all the time, which was a bit too much temptation for the kitties. Besides, it was against the law.

Bubba's story made it to the four-o'clock news with Diane Diaz. No one could believe that Bubba's parents would share child-care privileges with a human while raising a fledgling, that Wendy would give the bird flying lessons, or that a dog and cat assisted with the rescue. The newscast showed Bubba in his carrier case on a chair on the balcony, chirping like mad, waiting for his mum. Then they filmed Mum swooping down with a worm or a grub in her mouth, holding onto the cage door with her tiny feet, and feeding Bubba through the bars.

Papa bird always brought pretty flowers to feed his son. That showed that in the bird kingdom, the females were the warriors, and the males were more sensitive. A few birds lingered around the balcony on the telephone wires or in a tree, acting as sentries each day. We imagined those were Bubba's aunts and uncles.

It was amazing to watch nature in action. The crew followed Wendy into the bathroom, where Bubba executed his perfect flying lessons, always to land on her head or shoulder, then kiss her mouth. Ms. Diaz doing the interview loved the fact that Wendy named the mockingbird Bubba, because she had a son with that name.

I was proud the entire time and took it all in stride. Then came the day when Wendy, Angus, and I drove up to Tippi Hedren's wildlife station so Bubba could be rehabbed back into the wild. Angus cried more than Wendy when we left.

Bubba was a very healthy teenager. The animal services officer told us he would help other fledglings adapt. They put the birds into a darkened room for two weeks without any sounds, so they were deprogrammed from any influences of being tamed. In six weeks, the birds were taken to a specific area to be released into new habitat.

We understood that mockingbirds, blue jays, and some other bird species weren't released into their home areas. Those birds were very territorial, so that would start a war. Doves could be released with their families, proving that doves were appropriately named as the peace sign.

Bubba was a special little guy. We missed him like crazy and would always remember him. He was another miracle thanks to Wendy, me, and Decibel, the neighbor's kitty.

Libby wants to tell the rest of the story. "Like Bubba, Lovie Dovie, the dove I rescued, stayed with us for six-to-eight weeks before he was ready to be set free. Wendy, Savannah, and I drove to the wildlife station in Malibu. The people there told us the bird was a healthy teenager, and, like Bubba, would go through the same kind of rehab. Wendy was teary-eyed again, as she handed Lovie Dovie to the officer. We would miss that little guy. Every morning and evening, he had flying lessons. He always landed on Wendy's shoulder. He would have stayed with her all day if he could. He became a member of the family, loved by all. The officer patted my chest, too, and told me what a good rescue job I did."

13

Times They Are A-Changing

We began going to the dog park. It was becoming more of a habit after I started slowing down. We met our friend Bobbi Jo and her dog Buddy for a visit one day. Wendy found Buddy for Bobbi Jo through a rescue email. It seemed easier to just chill out with some other dogs, sniff, and exchange our "business cards" than my chasing after balls in the park.

We went at our usual time. Libby shot off like a horse at the starting gate, her head high, her tail sailing behind her. I loved watching her. She was in ecstasy, as if her spirit was released. She circled the park and finally went up to another little dog to exchange greetings.

I walked around, taking my time, sniffing everything in sight. I noticed a bigger dog eyeing Libby. He walked up to her slowly and sniffed her. She stopped and eagerly greeted the dog. He seemed nice enough.

The dog walked away. Libby, totally abashed, took off

for another race around the park. As she neared the big dog, he began to chase her. My senses picked up a red flag. She held her own, but the dog caught up and rolled her. I ran over to Libby, nosing her to make sure she was OK. The dog was up to something, and my blood curdled.

Wendy looked for the owner and saw a man standing there. "Is your dog friendly?"

"Oh, sure. He's fine. Just having fun."

I urged Libby to come visit Buddy with me. Libby took off like the Mad Hatter. Again, the dog chased her, but he seemed more aggressive. I was alert to it all and felt my body tense. Something wasn't cool, so I went over to cut them off when the big dog rolled Libby again with his teeth bearing down on her.

I bared my own teeth and charged just in time. We got into a fight. He was bigger, so I had to be careful where I tackled him.

Before I knew it, Wendy was yelling at the owner, telling him to grab his dog and pull him away by his tail. She did the same with me. She also had a bottle of water and was ready to pour it down my foe's face. If you get water into a dog's nose, it will force its mouth open if he won't let go any other way. Luckily, we weren't in that situation, though it was close.

I was mad. All I smelled was hostility. The man grabbed his dog, while Wendy pulled me back. She checked Libby and me to see if we'd been bitten. It was all over in a flash, thank God.

Libby, totally taken by surprise, never had that happen before. It scared her to pieces. She felt bad for me and promised she would be on guard from then on. She had learned her lesson.

The guy apologized, saying his dog never did that before. Other dog owners stood with us.

"This park is specifically for smaller dogs," one told him.

He promised not to bring his dog again. It was a near miss for Liberty. I was fine. It was awhile since I had had such an adrenalin rush.

"Your courageous soul leaped in there just in time to protect Libby," Wendy told me, "but this was almost too much for you, my girl."

It was true. I was too old for things like that, but I'd do anything for Libby. Wendy didn't want me in the position of having to jeopardize my own safety. I would give my life for my family, and Wendy knew it. She didn't want to take a chance.

Our doggie park days ended. We kept to our quiet walks around the neighborhood. There was plenty to do on those walks, with all the other neighbor dogs, cats, and friendly people who were glad to give loving pats and kisses. Once Libby trembled under me, terrified when other people approached. Now she changed into an outgoing social butterfly.

Hilary, our neighbor, had two cats, Pixie and Lucy. Wendy often took care of them when Hilary left town. She mentioned frequently that she wanted a dog someday. Hilary and Wendy became very close. She often went on walks with us, taking Libby's leash. Whenever Wendy was out of town, Hilary fed our kitty crew, while Carlos cared for Libby and me.

Libby took a shine to Marmaladee since the first day, and their bond grew deeper. In the spring of 2007, Marmaladee, Li'l Tyke, Guernsey May, and Elmo accepted Gini's kitty Cleo, a black long-haired beauty, into our fold. Wendy brought her to our home, because Gini's other cat, Sterling, was picking on her.

In November 2006, Wendy rescued Cleo from the East Valley Shelter. She was red-listed, which meant she would be euthanized the following day. She was a very sick little kitty and needed antibiotics for two months. Gini immediately adopted her. Wendy went to Gini's twice a day for two months to force food, water, and medication down her. It was touch-and-go, but she made it and became the sweetest little girl without a hiss in her vocabulary.

Wendy spoke to her pet psychic, Deb, about her, and she told Wendy that Cleo had given up and was ready to die. Those two months Wendy refused to give up, and it showed what persistence and love could do. We were lucky.

I was slowly losing my sight. I got around great, but the cataracts were obvious. My incontinence was hit-and-miss, more good days than bad but I had a healthy appetite and looked forward to my walks. I was still enamored when I saw a new kitty in the neighborhood, always ready to make a new friend.

My devotion to Libby was never-ending. I felt pressed to teach her everything I could, because I knew I was running out of time. Even though she was stronger and would soldier on to more-challenging occasions, Libby still had painful memories, and I wanted to make sure the rest of her life was trauma-free.

I slept a lot more and found it harder to wake up. Once Wendy tried to wake me, but I wouldn't. She picked me up, and I finally woke up to find her hugging me. I assured her I was OK with a big kiss, but I was tired.

Liberty Pearl's first photo!

"Libby" and Savannah

Savannah and Libby

Savannah and Libby

Libby

Savannah

Savannah & Liberty Pearl

Libby and Savannah

Bubba

Lovie Dovey

Maxamus "Maxamussy"

14

Saying Good Night to Savannah, Our Divine Daveene

On June 3, 2008, Wendy stayed home to be with Libby and me. She knew I would pass on soon. She spoke with her pet psychic for an hour, asking many questions, which I could have answered, but she wanted to assure herself she was doing the right thing. I felt bad. It was the worst waiting game ever.

She knew I was tired, becoming more and more lethargic and sad, yet I went on walks, gave her kisses, and tried to reassure her. That morning, I didn't even sniff my breakfast. Wendy was very concerned about Libby and how she would react to my passing. She was still very attached to me, so much so that Wendy felt she preferred my company to Wendy's. Sometimes, Wendy wondered if Libby cared that Wendy was in the same room.

How would Libby cope without me, her best friend, the one who taught her how to be a dog? Would Libby know that Wendy enabled my passing, if it came to it? There were many grueling thoughts.

🐾

Deb was kind, feeling Wendy's anguish, trying to comfort her the best she could. Wendy didn't have to call her, because she knew I would tell her when it was time.

That evening, I laid on the floor at Wendy's feet. Libby was restless. First, she was glued to my hind legs, her head on my rear end. Next she moved behind me, snuggling in as close as she could, her head on my back. Then Libby crawled between my legs, nestling against my tummy.

That went on all night. Finally, it was time for bed. Wendy started toward the stairs. Usually, the two of us followed her up the stairs, but I didn't move. I felt euphoric in dreamland. I wanted to get up, but my body was too heavy.

Wendy came to me and got on the floor to lie beside me. She held me, petting my head softly, saying how much she loved me. I looked at her and gently kissed her.

Wendy knew I wasn't going up the stairs with her. She considered staying on the couch to be with me, but I never slept on the bed or couch with Wendy and preferred to be on the floor at her side.

Something made her go upstairs to bed. It was me. I

told her it was OK, and she needed to let me go. There was nothing she could do. I was glad she understood. It killed me to let her go, and it killed her to leave me downstairs, but it was for the best.

We all needed to let go. Libby stayed with me. Wendy secretly prayed I would die peacefully in my sleep, but I wasn't quite ready to cross over.

On June 4, 2008, Wendy came downstairs and found Libby and me lying on the floor. I perked up when she saw me. I got up, wavered, and lay down again. Still, I was so alert, Wendy got a video camera and took a movie of Libby washing my face. We were all very happy. I looked at the camera with bright eyes. My spirit was so alive. Unfortunately, Wendy lost that video.

Suddenly, blood drained from my head. It was all I could do to stare at Wendy. She put down the camera and came to me, crying, as she scooped me into her arms. She was scared.

I didn't want her to be afraid. I wasn't. Libby knew she was going to lose me. My smell was different. Libby heard my heart beating fainter than usual. She was sad and felt helpless.

To keep busy, Libby kept cleaning my face, ears, and mouth. She didn't want to stop. She loved me deeply and didn't want to lose me. Instinctively, she knew our time together was almost over.

"What should I do?" Wendy asked. "Should I call the vet? Will she just pass gently in her sleep?"

Wendy started praying. Then she got the leashes and took us out for a walk. Somehow, I held my own and walked well.

"You're the most amazing dog," Wendy said. "You're so strong. You'll always be my Divine Daveene." "Divine Daveene" was Wendy's nickname for me, since I was so divine! I was determined to keep walking and refused to give up. We went to our favorite places and did our business quickly, then we returned to the house. Wendy prepared our breakfast and set it down. Libby scarfed hers. She was so concerned about me, she hadn't eaten much the previous night.

I walked away from my dish. It was my third day without eating or drinking.

"Savannah," Wendy asked, "are you telling me now?" She looked at Libby. It's funny what goes through your mind. You kind of play tricks on yourself. Of course, it's all a form of denial, not wanting to face the truth. You go in and out of the truth.

"I know, Savannah, your time is near, but I'm not God, and I'm not the one who should determine when you die, or am I? It's the cruelest thing on earth to be left with such a horrible decision, especially because you just walked and did your business so well, but you don't want food and water."

She collected her thoughts. "More important, how will Libby react? Libby, what will you do without your savior? I realize animals have natural instincts, and you're aware of

Savannah's slow decline, but how will it affect you when she's really gone?"

Weeks earlier, Wendy began a letter to Cesar Milan about this. Suddenly, an episode on Cesar's television show was specifically about the issue; how to help your dog when it loses its best doggie friend. She watched the show but was still worried, although she knew we had an unfathomable love that would never die.

In early afternoon, Wendy decided to take me for a walk without Libby. This would be my last walk. She wanted some alone time with me. We walked down the driveway. Again, I walked with a mission, feeling determined. We walked down the street to one of my favorite places, where I did my business.

We turned around to return home. Suddenly, I stopped walking and wavered on my feet. Wendy's heart throbbed. I couldn't move. Wendy picked me up. Once I had weighed fifty-two pounds, but by then I was around thirty-nine. She began crossing the street with me in her arms.

A man walked up and asked, "Are you OK?"

"Thank you," Wendy said softly. "My dog is dying."

She finally said it. *My dog is dying.* Hearing those words was like a bolt of lightning hitting both our hearts. However, she said it clearly, confirming the inevitable truth. I was dying.

When we walked back into the house, Libby was all over me, kissing me like I'd been missing for years. I immediately lay down, and Libby assumed her snuggly position behind me with her head on my rump.

"All I could do was stay by Savannah's side," Libby said later, "comforting her and loving her every single moment. She never stopped giving me love. Even in her last day, she made it clear I had to take care of Wendy and the kitties, be confident, and live in the security I created for myself over the last few years thanks to her."

I gathered more strength and said, "You are one bold dog, Liberty Pearl. Your spirit is unfathomable. You have your whole life ahead, and the world is yours. Trust in that and keep love in your heart, and you'll never go wrong. I love you, Little One. Thank you for teaching me more about life. You enriched my heart."

"I couldn't reply" Libby said later. "My eyes filled with tears as I lay on her rump, feeling her heartbeat become even fainter. I felt such gratitude and was overwhelmed with love. I knew she felt it, too. We took our final snooze together before we had to leave for the vet."

I looked at Wendy, not wanting to let her go. I always was a stubborn girl. My love and loyalty was more steadfast than the pain I felt, but I knew. I was exhausted. My gaze lost its focus. I stared into the distance, my body and mind somewhere else. My face changed slowly, as my body defied my mind.

I had to tell Wendy it was time.

Suddenly, Wendy wondered, *What if Savannah just has an infection? What if she's got a bug of some kind? Maybe we should see the vet.*

She quickly dialed the phone and made an appointment to come within the hour.

There she goes again, tricking herself, I thought. We always planned that the vet would come to our house, which he was willing to do, given all the years he's known me. Instead, she thinks she's taking me in for a checkup.

During the next half-hour, Wendy busied herself. I was drifting in and out. I needed to let Libby know I wouldn't be able to continue the story. We communicated with each other, and she knew I was making my transition.

I told Libby, I was passing the torch to her. I couldn't hold on any longer. I was slipping away.

Libby didn't answer. Her tail was tucked between her legs, and she knew I was already leaving.

On the drive to the vet, Wendy saw Woodbridge, my old park, on the left. She quickly got into the left lane, turned onto a side street and parked. She wanted to take me for one last visit.

She opened the back door and saw I was lying on the floor of the car. I had slid off the back seat where she placed me.

"Oh, my God!" she said. "What am I thinking? My baby's dying, and I'm taking her to the park?"

The mind is a crazy thing.

Wendy carried me into the vet's office. Everyone was expecting us and knew it was time to help me pass over the Rainbow Bridge. Had Wendy not tricked herself, we would never have gotten there.

We went into a room, and Libby came with us. She was very absorbed with me and my passing. Again, I told her to take care of Wendy.

"She'll need you without me here. I love you so much. Keep being courageous. You're the best little friend I ever had."

Those were my last words.

Libby continues: Even the death I saw in Iraq never prepared me to lose my Savannah. She treated me like a star, but <u>she</u> was the real guiding light. It was too painful. We all know what happens. All I can say is that Savannah basically passed away once she was laid on the table, not even needing the needle, though the shot helped her cross over more quickly and peacefully.

Wendy held her, kissing her face, telling her how much she loved her, how grateful that she chose us to spend her life with, and how our lives would never be the same without her. It was OK for her to go. And Wendy added that she and I would be OK. Wendy had almost eighteen years with that beautiful girl, our Divine Daveene.

"Her heart's still beating," Wendy told the vet. "Her heart is beating!"

He shook his head. Wendy realized it was her own heartbeat she heard and felt.

Dr. Schwartz left us to have time with her. Wendy held Savannah's body tightly and prayed.

I sat quietly and patiently, wanting to be next to Savannah. As I thought that, Wendy bent down to pick me up and placed me beside Savannah. I licked Savannah's mouth, kissing her, then her eyes. She was very still. My heart cried out, and my soul felt empty. Tears streamed down Wendy's face onto me and Savannah. I felt her warm hand on my back

I looked into Wendy's devastated face and felt nothing but love. I realized she was my mom. I had to trust she would take care of me. My best friend was gone. I no longer needed to care for Savannah. I needed to take care of Wendy.

Savannah told me to care for Wendy, and that was what I'd do. It was my new job.

I didn't remember how long we stayed with Savannah. I just remember it was all we could do to leave her.

Someone from the vet's office called Wendy's dad to tell him about Savannah's passing. They knew how close Wendy and her dad were and how much he loved Savannah.

Angus insisted on seeing Wendy and invited us to his condo, where we were joined by Gini and two other friends. We spent two hours crying and laughing together, remembering our best moments with Savannah and loving the fact of being together.

☸

Just three weeks earlier, Wendy had been in New York, staying with Gale, a close friend. Gale was visiting Los Angeles, and they had planned to meet for dinner on Wednesday, June 4.

Wendy had a dream about a week earlier and told Gale about it. In the dream, she was to meet Gale at seven o'clock, the time they agreed to in real life. Like some dreams, it turned into a nightmare. For some reason, Wendy was late, and she tried to get dressed but couldn't decide what to wear. She kept going through her closet, becoming increasingly frantic.

Then she realized she had to shower and wanted to wash her hair. By then it was 6:30, and she knew she'd be late, but she hopped into the shower, anyway. When she left the shower, she called Gale to say she would be late, arriving at her house around eight or nine, and apologized.

Gale said that would be too late, so Wendy pleaded with her and offered to leave in five minutes.

While sitting at her dad's condo, Wendy looked at the

clock and saw it was already six o'clock. She called Gale to say our beloved Savannah passed, and she'd be late, because she had to run home and change before we drove out to Malibu. She hugged her dad and friends, said good-bye and we left.

We hurried home, where she fed me, the kitties, changed, and then we drove to Gale's home in Malibu around eight. When she walked in, Gale smiled at me.

"So this is Liberty Pearl," Gale said. "How adorable."

I rolled on my back and looked at Gale sideways. I gave more of a look of surrender, as if saying, *OK, I'm getting used to this.*

Gale hugged Wendy. "Do you remember the dream you had? It's eight o'clock."

"Oh, my God," Wendy said. "How surreal is this?"

We all freaked out a little. Gale and Wendy got out glasses of wine and toasted Savannah many times.

Wendy and I spent the night there, too numb to move. She didn't want to go home without Savannah just yet. Hilary took care of the kitties.

Somehow, we slept. Maybe we were that exhausted. The past week was rough, knowing we were losing Savannah and worrying how it would turn out. I lay close to Wendy and stayed with her all night. This was new to me as I always slept next to Savannah on our big bed on the floor.

I woke to find Wendy staring at me. I kissed her face. I knew we faced a huge shift, but I was taking it well. Wendy and I grew even closer. I couldn't have asked for more. Warmth and love for each other filled our hearts. We would get through it. We felt Savannah's presence. The love was very strong. She was watching over us.

🐾

Later that morning, one of Wendy's best friends, Kathy told us to stop at her house on the way home from Gale's. Kathy had the sweetest dog named Layla, who gave me many kisses when we arrived. Layla sensed my sadness and entertained me by showing me her toys.

We stayed for the day and had dinner. After Wendy cried a few more tears, she felt ready to go home. She realized our house wouldn't be empty with all the precious critters waiting.

Wendy told me my character had blossomed. I was displaying more confidence and wasn't bolting. I didn't tremble as often, even when visiting strange new places, which was a huge step.

That night, I slept beside Wendy, as did all five kitties.

🐾

The next morning, Wendy went to the front door to get my collar and leash. Savannah's collar and leash hung on the doorknob. We both felt knots in our throats. Wendy lifted Savannah's collar and held it close, smelling it while tears ran down her cheeks. Our Divine Daveene was gone. We were blessed to have had her for so many years. She was almost eighteen, unheard of for a large dog.

Wendy calmed down and felt gratitude in her heart. She looked at me as I was wagging my tail. I loved how I felt and what I heard. Wendy realized the movement of Savannah's collar made a jingling sound, as the nametag, license, and Saint Agnes medal bounced off each other.

Wendy held the collar high and shook it. I wagged even harder. Then she placed Savannah's collar around her own neck, buckled on my collar and leash, and we left.

There was more strength in our pace, and we felt peaceful. It was as if Savannah walked with us. Wendy wore that collar for our walks every day for about a month. From it we designed a new jewelry line for pets and pet owners. We named the company Savannah Liberty.

15

Reflections on Savannah's Legacy

After Savannah left, I thought about all the things she had taught me. I tried to remember the events from the first ten months of my life, before I met Savannah and Wendy, but I couldn't. It was a blur. Obviously, I blanked it all out. Still, there was a sense of fear within me. Savannah urged me not to allow my thoughts and fears to linger any further than the first image that came. She said to see just that moment and quickly turn my nose upwind, take a deep sniff, and be in the new moment. I had to "be" wherever my nose scented. She promised to nudge me gently into the moment if I needed help.

Then she pushed me gently with her cold, wet nose to remind me we were sharing a beautiful moment together.

I looked deeper into her eyes, begging to hear more. I felt very safe. She told me there was no time other than the present. Anything else was a false scent. It might seem real, making the body tremble, but whatever triggered that sense brought up fearful moments from the past. It was like the garbage trucks coming up our alley. Savannah still had bad moments, herself, about the first times she heard the trucks and couldn't stop herself from telling the trucks how she felt. But her fear diminished over time. It became a memory of something that no longer existed. Only if we believed in that moment would it become the truth of right now.

Savannah's being in the moment became my new mantra. After all, weren't dogs all about being in the present? Ever since I moved in with Savannah, Wendy, the kitties, and the birds, I felt nothing but love surrounding me. Love became my wings and only purpose.

Each morning when I awoke, Savannah gently washed my face, motivating me to walk gallantly out the front door. It took a couple years for me not to have my tail down between my legs, but I slowly began to understand.

Savannah gave me confidence to meet each day and accept whatever it offered. Wendy had a lot to do with it, too. She gave constant words of praise. I could do no wrong. She wanted to cuddle more than I liked. I was never a snuggler, but I loved it when Wendy scratched my tummy. Even with that, though, I had a limit.

However, I loved cuddling with Savannah. There wasn't a safer, more comfortable place on earth. Her breathing soothed me, her heart beating with mine. We were in sync, and I never wanted to move.

My best friend was gone. I knew Wendy was concerned

about me and how I would react. I was, too. When I sensed Savannah declining, my heart sank to its lowest depths. We had only four years together, and it passed so quickly. I wasn't ready for her to leave, even though we animals understand that this life is fleeting. We instinctively accept that.

Still, that didn't take away the pain and longing for more time together. People say that dogs have no sense of time, but we understand mortality and loss. I knew I was losing Savannah. I remained strong even when picking up on Wendy's sadness. Because Wendy was being strong, so I found myself being strong. I did better than I thought I would.

16

After Savannah, More Rescue

Our days were now spent traveling here and there. Wendy stayed busy with her dance company teaching. The rest of the summer, she was obsessed with creating Savannah Liberty's new jewelry design, but something was missing.

Obviously, we both missed our girl Savannah. Wendy was concerned for me, though I seemed all right. I wasn't eating as enthusiastically, and my tail was low most of the time. I kept my daily routine of bathing Elmo and Marmaladee, but I was quiet and a bit lethargic.

At the end of July, Wendy woke up one day with a strong, almost-overwhelming compulsion to visit the East Valley Animal Shelter. That was the high-kill shelter where she originally found Savannah, Guernsey May, Cleo, and Chewey. Wendy felt an urge to rescue a deserving soul in Savannah's name.

I thought it was a great idea. I would love some

company. We would foster a dog until we found it the perfect home.

The shelter was brimming with activity. A woman held a stray cat in a carrier and handed it to someone at the reception desk. Wendy saw that and felt terrible to see a poor animal being put into the system. We already had five cats, and we didn't dare rescue another. Besides, Wendy wanted a dog.

She walked up and down the corridors, past kennels filled with dogs. Some had three or four in them. Our reception was overwhelming with a chorus of barking and whining.

How could she choose? There were so many. Wendy usually looked for the underdogs, the ones listed green or red. Green meant a dog was only days from being red-listed. A red listing meant the dog would be euthanized within a day.

Then Wendy fell in love with a large, eighty-pound pure-white Pitbull/American Bulldog that had been "owner surrendered." She was almost an albino and had boundless energy filled with love and kisses. She could hardly contain herself when Wendy showed her affection.

She was in a kennel with two other Pits, which was a good sign that she got along with other dogs. Wendy immediately named her Snow White. She also saw a lovely Blue Pit named Beyonce that had also been "owner surrendered." She sat calmly at the front of her kennel, giving Wendy kisses.

Nearby, a brown Pit lay at the ground at the front of his kennel, as if waiting for his owner. That one, too, was "owner surrendered." His collar hung on a nail outside the kennel. Wendy called him Taboo.

Then on the final round among the kennels, Wendy saw the most handsome dog with soulful eyes. He slowly moved toward her and turned his face against the chain-link fence, so she could rub his ear. That was what Savannah did the first time they met. He looked like a male counterpart of Savannah, like a refined Gordan Setter, maybe with a little Bernese mountain dog.

He was a gorgeous dog. His info showed he was green-listed, having been brought in as a stray. He'd been hit by a car and just had hip surgery. It always amazed me that people at an animal shelter would save an animal's life, perhaps perform surgery. Then, if the animal wasn't adopted, they would euthanize it.

Wendy had to choose. She was allowed to put a hold on animals, but only three at a time. She put a hold on Snow White, Beyonce, and the noble boy she called Prince.

That night, she spent hours on the internet and phone, trying to locate a dog-rescue group that would help out.

"I must have lost my mind," she told me. "I can rescue all three if I find temporary lodging for the two Pits."

She didn't know how they'd react to cats and me, a much-smaller dog. We lived in a small place that had a tiny patio that wouldn't accommodate Snow White's massive energy. We must've had a guardian angel, perhaps Savannah, watching over us that night, because we found someone for Beyonce and Snow White.

The following day, Wendy took the girls to the rescue group and took Prince to a vet for a check-up. She visited Taboo and told him she'd take him home the next day.

After picking up Prince, she got home around 6:45. She immediately called the shelter to confirm that Taboo was being held for us.

"I'm sorry," the receptionist said. "What's the dog's number?"

Wendy gave her the number.

"I'm sorry, but that dog was euthanized."

"That can't be. I was just there and put a hold. When was he put down?"

"He was taken to the clinic fifteen minutes ago."

"Can you call them? Maybe it's not too late!"

"I'm sorry, Miss, but it's too late. The dog was euthanized."

All Wendy could think of was that darling dog, lying on his outstretched paws, staring at the door and waiting for someone to take him home, his collar waiting just above his head. She cried, and we said a prayer for Taboo, asking him to forgive Wendy. He was another loving soul lost in the shuffle, but at least he was loved.

I was at the front door, all excited, when Wendy opened it.

"Yes, Libby, there's someone for you to meet," she said.

I followed her outside to the car, where Prince waited in a crate. She put a leash on him and brought him out to meet me. Prince's tail wagged like crazy. I made little cries of joy.

He was stunning and had such good vibes. I kissed him, as if I'd known him for years. He did the same for me. It seemed like Savannah was doing her magic.

We went for our first walk. I was eager to show him all our favorite places. I couldn't believe how Prince slipped in like the royal angel he was. He walked a little ahead, then turned around to eye me, waiting for me to catch up. He nosed me as if to ask, "All good? Let's go."

It was a perfect match. My spirits rose, and soon, I was back to my normal self.

🐾

That night, we sat on the patio to enjoy the warm summer evening. Prince just wanted to be loved. Wendy couldn't stop petting him and noticed he was sensitive around the hip after what he'd gone through. He was about a year old.

"Where'd you come from, Boy?" she asked.

Wherever it was, he showed no sign of ill treatment. If anything, he'd been loved. How did he end up getting hit by a car? Did he escape his yard? He didn't seem like a dog that would run off or wander. Was he dumped? No one came to look for him at the shelter. It made us wonder.

Meanwhile, I snuggled up to him, as I did with Savannah. Prince didn't seem to mind, but I stayed away from his bad hip.

The following morning, Wendy planned to take Prince to an adoption set up by a rescue group she knew. Our heartstrings tugged at us. She knew she was in love with Prince, and I loved him, too. He was the perfect fit, even with all the kitties. Wendy still mourned Savannah and felt it was too soon for us.

She took us on a nice walk. Wendy's heart sank, as she watched Prince walk side-by-side with me. Should we keep him? My heart said, "Yes," but I knew that Mom knew best, and I had to go along with her decision.

Once she was at the adoption, Wendy felt she was doing the right thing. Prince reminded us so much of Savannah. Maybe someone would have the amazing life with Prince that we did with Savannah.

Wendy began to change her mind and was about to leave and take Prince home when two men walked toward her. They were impressed by Prince's story of surviving the accident and the animal shelter. They were interested and said they'd go for coffee while they made up their minds.

Wendy took Prince for a walk. She was in trouble, because she loved him. Then she thought of his hip and how he might need more surgery or have complications. We weren't in a good financial state, and she wanted what was best for Prince.

The men returned, and the one named Colin said he wanted Prince. He took the leash from Wendy, and the two of them walked toward the office to fill out the necessary paperwork.

Suddenly, with horrible barking and a screech, Prince jumped up hitting Wendy's back with his front paws. He was agitated, wanting to stay by Wendy's side.

She fought back tears. Could it be we'd become that attached in twenty-four hours? What should we do? Wendy tried to imagine Prince and me together.

"I'll take good care of him," Colin said. "I'll take him to see my vet tomorrow."

Wendy gave him the paperwork, which he filled out, then volunteered to bring Prince to Colin's house. Crying the whole way, she took Prince to his new home.

On the ride, she talked quietly to Prince, telling him how much she loved him and how he'd be in good hands. He sat quietly in the back seat, staring at her.

Once at the house, Wendy inspected it and the yard to make sure it was secure. Colin had a smaller dog that was slow at meeting Prince. Prince remained quiet, seeming a bit confused, but he was smart. Colin and Wendy agreed to set up a play date once things were settled, but it never happened.

Wendy left that night feeling drained and empty. She felt she might have let me down, too. Maybe it was the wrong decision, but she knew Prince would have good care, and he did. But we always thought Prince was the dog we let get away.

After Prince, I adjusted fine. The rescue group that helped with Prince's adoption gave us a dog to take home to foster that same evening. I greeted him joyfully and gave him a tour. We called him Charley Bear. He had a new home a week later.

Then there was Jake, who went to an adoring family, and Izzie, who a neighbor adopted. Over time, Wendy placed Beyonce in a wonderful home. Bey became a therapy dog, educating people about her breed and what good dogs Pits really were and how loving they could be.

It took over two years to find Snow White a perfect home. She moved to Utah. All those fosters were a success, and I thrived on the company. It kept me busy, and my tail was always up.

Of course, I still played with Chewey when we visited Gini. I had plenty of fun with orphaned friends staying over who were more than happy to play. I had a purpose, inviting temporarily homeless critters in. I taught them everything Savannah taught me and more. I demonstrated where courage came from and told them to trust in the unknown. I was coming more out of my shell. Wendy swore I was laughing at times.

17

Liberty's New Best Friend, Sam

It was mid-November. Wendy and I got through the summer months and fall pretty well. We rescued, fostered, and found homes for over ten dogs. We also rescued two bunnies and a litter of four kittens, all of which found homes, too. Winter was coming on, as much as anyone could say that about Los Angeles.

Gini's dog walker and Wendy's new friend, Tatiana, just lost two of her Pit Bulls, which died within months of each other. One day, Wendy mentioned a pregnant Pit to Tatiana, who was at the Downy Shelter, another high-kill shelter. She saw a photo of the dog and immediately wanted to meet her.

They had to hurry to get to the Pit before she had her puppies. Once she had her litter, they'd have to pay for all the newborns, too.

They went in late afternoon and met Hazel. She was an adorable white and beige dog, no more than ten months old. She bulged with her imminent delivery. As Tatiana took care of the adoption procedure, Wendy was escorted through the shelter. Though Wendy remained private about it, her name had come out as being a rescuer. She was shown dozens of Pits, mixes, and puppies. Her heart was torn at seeing all the homeless babies and knowing many would die from illness or euthanasia.

Toward the end of the tour, she saw a lovely Dalmatian peering out of his cage and stopped to say hello. Then she saw a dark shadow behind him with two auburn eyes staring at her. It was a pure-black dog with slight white markings. He put his nose to the fence and let her look at him. When she placed her hand near him, he sniffed it and turned his head sideways to have his ear scratched.

He looked at her, backed up a bit, and sat down as if asking, "Well?"

That was the same greeting Savannah gave Wendy almost eighteen years earlier. Wendy felt a sense of peace come over her. The dog was calm and handsome, a Lab/Husky/Shepherd mix of some kind.

Wendy smiled at him, secretly saying she'd be seeing him again.

As Tatiana finished her paperwork, Wendy asked about some of the puppies she met and put a hold on the handsome dog she had just made a vow to herself to see again. All would be safe for the time being until Wendy made some calls.

Wendy and Tatiana led the happy, tail-wagging, ready-to-burst Hazel from the shelter to the car. They were worried she'd give birth in the car, so they brought a blanket and towels just in case.

They made it to Tatiana's house and showed Hazel her new home. Wendy left the happy couple and drove home.

As soon as she came inside, she told me the story about the handsome black dog she met and how she planned to foster him.

"One more dog, Libby," she said. "Just one more."

Two days later, we took the long drive down to the Downey Shelter to rescue Mr. Handsome. I waited in the car, filled with anticipation.

An officer took the dog from his kennel to a grassy, enclosed area where people could meet dogs without cages. Mr. Handsome was very low-key and humble. He let Wendy pet him all over and offered his paw. The officer told her he'd been brought in with his white brother as "owner surrendered." His name was Hawk. The dogs were young puppies.

The white one was adopted fairly quickly, but Mr. Handsome stayed in the back of the shelter for at least six months.

Six months? I wondered. *How did he survive in a high-kill shelter that long? Why was he kept in the back where no one could see him? Was he red-listed?*

None of it made sense. But Wendy and I were grateful that we found him when we did.

Mr. Handsome was an amazing animal. He couldn't have been gentler or sweeter. More aggressive dogs walked past him with officers holding their leashes tightly, but Mr. Handsome just looked at them and remained calm. He wagged his tail for some of the passersby, but he seemed on high alert with Wendy, giving her all his attention. The name Hawk spoke for itself.

Wendy took a picture of him. He was truly a regal dog. The same rescue group that backed Wendy for Prince agreed to back her for Mr. Handsome. That meant she could pull him out under their name and give him his tags. She would be allowed to show the dog at the rescue group's adoption days.

Wendy finished the paperwork and was ready to take him when the shelter officer said it wouldn't be until the next day, because he had to be neutered. She never hit that snag before, because she usually took a dog or cat to her own vet to be neutered. That place had different rules.

The next day was Thanksgiving Eve. Traffic would be horrific, so Wendy asked Gini to come along. I planned to come, too, so I could get a good sniff of our new friend on the way home. Wendy would keep Mr. Handsome in his crate until we could meet in our driveway.

I was excited once we arrived at the shelter. Wendy went to the officer to finalize the paperwork and was told,

"Oh, he was already neutered. You could have taken him yesterday."

She sighed.

After dropping Gini off at her home, we arrived at our own driveway. I kept making soft whimpering sounds. I couldn't wait to meet our new friend. He had a delicious scent. Wendy finally let me sniff close to the crate. Mr. Handsome enjoyed that and made a little playful bark. Wendy let him out, and he and I danced around each other, sniffing everywhere. I did my famous roll onto my back but without the wish to die, rather to let him know he was dominant over me. I was grinning. Then I jumped to Handsome's mouth and kissed him like crazy. He nudged me and threw his rear end at me. He towered over me, so I couldn't see, but I knew instant love.

We immediately went for a walk, and Mr. Handsome had the same respect and concern for me as Prince had. He'd get a little ahead, pause, and look back to see if I was still following.

"What a good boy, eh, Libby?" Wendy asked. "Reminds me of Prince, doesn't he?"

I looked up and agreed 100 percent. Somehow, the name Hawk didn't fit this dog. True, he was extremely sharp. His radar was up constantly, and he never missed anything. He was more intense than any dog I had known before, but he didn't seem completely like a hawk.

Then his new name came out without Wendy having to think about it. "Sam, how do you like the neighborhood?"

He turned toward her as if he'd heard that name for years. I wagged my tail.

"Sam? Sammy? Do you prefer that over Hawk?"

He came to Wendy and nosed her leg, then kissed me. We took that as his answer. He was Sam.

The next day was Thanksgiving. We planned to have it at Gini's home and had quite a few people coming. Sam and I came, too. Wendy was concerned about how Chewey would accept Sam. Chewey still showed his dislike of big dogs whenever we went for walks. If one dared come toward him, he didn't waste any time telling that dog off. Wendy was a lot sterner with him when she had his leash, so he didn't go as ballistic. Gini had a softer touch and didn't keep up with the training.

Gini wanted to meet Sam. Besides, it was part of Chewey's ongoing training. We arrived early that afternoon to help set the table and prepare side dishes. Gini had a young friend staying with her, helping out with meals and daily activities. He was working on the turkey.

When we arrived, Wendy had Gini meet us outside with Chewey. That always worked better, so Chewey wouldn't feel imposed on in his own space. Chewey became excited when he saw Wendy and me, then he froze and remained quiet. Wendy let Sam and Chewey sniff each other face-to-face for three seconds, then she stepped back. There was still no barking.

Hmmm, I thought. *This is going well.*

We walked up the street without any commotion and returned to Gini's home. Gini kept Chewey on his leash, as Wendy kept Sam.

They sat at opposite sides of the table. The evening was going well until they removed the leashes during dessert. We made it through to the final cup of coffee when suddenly Chewey went after Sam. They made a lot of noise.

Wendy got up only to see Sam calmly walking away, with Chewey still after him. She grabbed Chewey and calmed him down. The leashes were put back on.

Oh, well, I thought. *So much for this working out.*

Wendy was determined to help Chewey through his defensive moments. Sam seemed like the perfect candidate, because he didn't fight back and wasn't daunted by the ordeal. Was he just on good behavior? It seemed to us that if he wanted to fight back, he would have. He was so gentle with me and Chewey, so Wendy decided to make that a positive, and we would get through Chewey's Hitler-hood.

The following weekend, Wendy wasn't very keen to take Sam to an adoption day. She made up an excuse to stay away on Saturday and Sunday by visiting friends and bringing us along. Her friends loved Sam at first sight and enjoyed how gentle he was with me.

"He's yours," they said, "yours and Libby's."

Wendy still wasn't sure. Maybe she felt it was too soon after Savannah's passing. She thought Sam needed a family that had a house with a big yard. With his size, he needed more space than we could offer at a townhouse with a small outdoor patio.

Then a friend reminded her that Savannah lived in an apartment with her for years and was fine. We lived across from Woodbridge Park back then and visited the park three or four times a day.

Wendy remained undecided.

One morning, as Wendy was getting off the phone, she felt upset by an unpleasant conversation. Recently, she had been having health issues including bronchitis and asthma that led to panic attacks. Once again, it seemed we had mold in our townhouse, just like back in the old apartment.

"Mold must like me," Wendy said.

As soon as she hung up, though, she began to have trouble breathing. She tried to calm herself, but nothing worked. She gasped and began to panic. When she stood up, Sam immediately came to her and stood up with his front paws around her waist, trying to pull her down.

I watched as he suddenly became forceful enough to bring her down. She backed up to the couch and lay on her back. Sam jumped up with her and placed his body between her legs, with his chest lying on hers, and his face against hers. His front paws stretched over her shoulders.

"No, Sam," she said. "Not now. No kisses. I can't breathe."

He began taking slow, deliberate breaths against her face. He refused to budge. He kept up that slow breathing for a while, and she suddenly realized she was breathing *with* him, taking slow, deliberate breaths herself.

Oh, my God, Wendy thought. *What is he doing? How did he know how to do this?*

When she felt better and was more relaxed, she wrapped her arms around Sam's strong back and thanked him. "You're a keeper, Sam. You aren't going anywhere. Right, Libby?"

We couldn't believe it. We had a healer in our household! Wendy was so grateful.

I was on the floor, looking up at Wendy sternly. *I told you he's supposed to be here,* I was saying to her. *He's ours, and we're his. It's about time you got it.*

She got it, all right. We all had each other from then

on. Sam, with further training, became Wendy's service dog shortly after that episode.

Instantly, I bonded with Sam as I had with Savannah. I lay in his paws against his belly with my head on his rump. I hid under him whenever I felt shy or insecure on our walks, and I followed him everywhere. He loved it. He immediately fit in with our daily schedule, going for car rides to be at Gini's, assisting Wendy while she taught her classes. Everything Savannah and I once did, Sam and I did. He was Savannah's male counterpart.

He turned out to be a very good dog. He automatically did his business outside without a single mistake. He came and sat on command. Wendy enrolled him in dog training, and soon he was taking agility classes. He was amazing. He watched other dogs go through the program. Then, when it was his turn, he copied what he saw. He had to learn how to weave through the poles, but running through tubes, jumping through tires, and getting on the table came automatically, as if he'd done them in a past life.

I watched and barked him on, feeling very proud of him. I told him I refused to break a claw doing such things, because they weren't for me.

When the agility class ended, I ran up to give Sam kisses, prancing around him. It was as if he won the Olympic Marathon.

Sam at Downey Shelter the first day we met. "Chewey" bacca

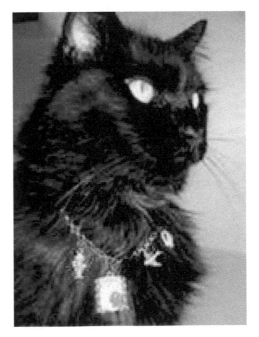

Cleo

Li'L Tyke & Marmaladee

Elmo

Guernsey May aka "Gothie Kitty"

Liberty Pearl and her friends...

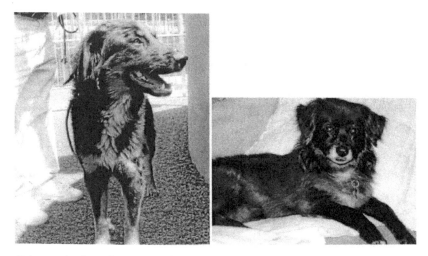

Prince who later became "Simon"   *Jake*

Snow White   Beyonce

Jasper

Kevin

Josh and Cathy

18

Elmo and Li'l Tyke

The following year was tough. At the end of June, 2009, Elmo, our diabetic kitty, suddenly lost a lot of weight and was weakening. Wendy rescued him in December, 2005. He was believed to be ten at that time, but who really knew? We grew close to him, he had such a precious personality.

Wendy gave him insulin shots twice a day, and he never complained. He greeted her each time with a loving snuggle and purr. He touched his paw to her face when they were close. He fell into a crease in her heart and into mine.

We hated to see it happening, but there was no denying he was in poor shape. Wendy walked the dogs one day and thought she'd take Elmo to the vet when she returned.

"Please," a voice told her, "no more vets or needles or probing. I just want to stay home."

She acknowledged the plea and respected it. Elmo was dying, and he wanted it to be peaceful. She arranged to have bags of saline at home to keep him hydrated, and she offered him baby food or anything he could stomach.

On July 7th Sam started jumping on the couch and pawing at Wendy. He snuggled his head into her hand and lay beside her. I was worried. I smelled something off, but I didn't know what it could be. I jumped on the couch beside him to snuggle and get a better sense.

Wendy knew something was wrong. Sam looked sad and quiet, and he kept pawing her.

Is this because of Elmo? I wondered.

We planned to go to Laguna Beach that weekend and stay with friends, but those plans were on hold due to Elmo. Now it seemed something was wrong with Sam.

Wendy called the vet for an appointment for Sam hopefully to rule anything out. It turned out Sam had Parvo, a serious disease that killed most dogs, especially puppies. It was contagious.

I wasn't worried, because I had all my shots, but I was scared for Sam. Dr. Schwartz said it was a mild case, but that Sam had to be hospitalized.

That happened on Friday. Around noon on Saturday, Wendy took me out for a walk. As soon as we came to the end of the first block, Wendy heard a voice that said, "You need to turn around and go home *now.*"

We returned and walked into the kitchen to find Elmo on the kitchen floor. Wendy joined him and held him. I kissed Elmo, while tears rolled off Wendy's face. Elmo turned his head toward Wendy, meowed once, and took his last breath. His head lay in her hand, her arms around his frail body.

Wendy's friends encouraged her to get away with me and come to Laguna. Sam was in the hospital, and there was nothing we could do. Elmo passed and went to the angels, so Wendy and I took off.

It was our first outing on our own since Savannah passed. Wendy was curious to see how I behaved. She wondered if my trembling would return or my old insecurities might resurface. Unfortunately, my shyness did take over.

When we met Wendy's friends, John and Jeanie, I promptly rolled on my back with the ol' "step on me and get it over with" look. When we walked down the sidewalks, I was skittish and trembling.

We decided to return home early, where I felt safe. I missed Sam. Jeanie and John always talked softly and sweetly to me. Jeanie seemed determined to get to know me. Finally, I allowed her to pick me up and put me on the couch between her and Wendy, as she gently massaged my tummy. It felt good, but I was still uneasy.

After three minutes, I sniffed and licked Jeanie's hand and jumped off the couch to lie at Wendy's feet. At least that was progress. I appeared more relaxed the following day, staying close to Wendy. She wondered if my trembling and skittishness would ever go away.

I'd been through a lot. I felt like PTSD was my middle name, but the trip was good for me, too. I had the chance to gain more trust and confidence. I could always before rely on Savannah and Sam, but was that a good thing? Didn't I need to feel more secure on my own and build my confidence to avoid feeling so fearful? I was better than when Wendy first got me. My tongue no longer hung out all the time, and I didn't bolt when someone picked me up. I was more like a jumping bean, not bolting manically.

No matter how long it took or how difficult it was, I knew Wendy and Sam were there for me. By the end of the weekend, I was thanking both Jeanie and John with plenty of kisses.

"The love that comes from this little dog is abundant," John said.

Love is healing. I swear it saved my life and would always get me through. I had plenty of love to give.

🐾

We couldn't wait to pick up Sam. He recovered beautifully and was thrilled to be back home. Once I stopped giving him kisses, he had to investigate the house and make sure the kitties were still there and everything was OK.

He sniffed at the floor where Elmo passed, and I joined him.

"Yes, Sam," Wendy said. "Elmo's gone. He went over the Rainbow Bridge and is with Savannah and Maxamussy now."

He seemed to understand and went to drink water from his bowl.

·.·

In the summer, Wendy received a call from a fellow rescuer with an emergency. Three small terriers needed an immediate foster.

"Could we?" Wendy asked me. "Would we?"

I accepted. Wendy said she did, too, almost without thinking.

She picked up the trio. One was pure black and tiny, so we named him MJ for Michael Jackson, who had just passed. The second little guy was adorable, and we named him Scout. The third guy looked just like Scruffy, so that was it.

We made introductions to me, Sam, and the kitties. All went well. MJ and Scout found homes quickly, and Scruffy attached himself to Wendy. I wasn't jealous. He was a sweet little fella.

A month later, a lady said she'd take him. Within two days, she called back to return him. Her dog didn't like Scruffy.

Wendy picked up Scruffy and brought him home. He was nothing but a gentleman at our house. Sam and I welcomed him back with sniffs and kisses. Three months later we found him the perfect family.

·.·

January 17, 2010 was yet another very sad day for all of us. It greatly affected Wendy and all of us critters. We visited Gini that day. It made Wendy gloomy. Gini was still able to make a few social gatherings, but it was becoming more and more difficult. She stayed home a lot more and was declining. Some days Wendy just sobbed. I tried my best to comfort her by being silly in the hope of making her smile. Sam, Chewey, and I sensed a change in Gini.

🐾

That evening Wendy had gone out. When she came home Sam, Scruffy, and I ran to her as usual, but that time was different. I was a nervous wreck, and Sam was agitated.

"Hi, Guys." Wendy went right to her phone, which had many messages. I went to lie on the kitchen floor to watch her. Sam and Scruffy went in and out of the dog door.

Wendy was listening to her messages when she realized we were acting funny, all of us restless. She looked outside to see if we had a kitty from the neighborhood visiting, which happened occasionally, or maybe a baby possum was roaming around.

She didn't see anything for a moment, then she froze when she noticed a white blob. She couldn't see too well through the glass as it was raining, so she opened it and saw Li'l Tyke lying there without moving. When she came closer, she saw he had passed on.

Li'l Tyke was hypothyroid and on medication. Often,

though, I found the pill she gave him on the ground. He hated taking it and was very clever when he spit it out.

She had Li'l Tyke since he was five weeks old. She adopted Maxamussy the same day, when Max was six weeks old, giving him the name after Maximus from the *Gladiator*. She saw that movie the day she brought the kitten boys home.

Li'L Tyke became one of her favorites. It wasn't easy to admit she had favorites. That made her feel guilty, but everyone had favorites. He was a little rascal, full of fun, who made her laugh. He never got over suckling, and Wendy was his mommy. From his first days with her, he spat on her arm and rolled his nose in it until he found the right spot to begin nursing. That was what little kittens did with their mom, rolling their noses through the fur until they found the nipple. With his tongue smacking the roof of his mouth, he made little "tsah, tsah" sounds and began sucking like crazy while kneading her arm. He did that every morning when Wendy woke up, including the morning of the day he died.

Wendy still weeps for him. I miss him too. She wishes she'd been with us that night, as he passed. Nature has its own course, as tragic and unfair as it might seem.

Two weeks later, as Wendy walked down the townhouse

stairs, she heard a voice say, "I'll be back as soon as I can."

꙳

Wendy wondered how I was taking the loss of Elmo and Li'l Tyke. She knew animals mourned for losses, and she saw me keep going, especially after Savannah's passing.

She sensed something, though, because I wasn't feeling quite right those days. My tail was low for almost a week now, and I wasn't keen to have morning treats. Then I suddenly lost weight until my ribs were easily felt.

Wendy planned to take me to the vet the first thing the next day. That afternoon, though, I lay trembling on the floor. I wasn't scared. It was totally different. I felt weak and a strange floating sensation. Later, I was told I might have had a mild seizure.

Wendy, finding me lying on the floor, gravely concerned, rushed me to the vet.

After many tests and days of discussion with Dr. Schwartz, he concluded I had Addison's disease. It could be hereditary or brought on by stress. The latter seemed most probable. My introduction to life and the first year and a half would have given anyone a heart attack, let alone Addison's disease. Then I lost Savannah, Maxamussy, Elmo, and Li'l Tyke.

It made sense. They put me on a regiment of Prednisone daily and a Percorten shot every twenty-one days. Wendy wanted to know more about the disease and investigated it. She contacted UC Davis, known for the best animal studies by veterinarians in the country, and spoke to a doctor.

She told him she was worried about giving me all those steroids, and she was concerned about the long-term effects. For the past few months, she'd been giving me a quarter tab of Prednisone every other day, and the Percorten shot every six weeks. Sam accompanied me whenever I had a shot. He was my emotional support. My blood tests were looking great, and I was thriving. I felt well.

The doctor agreed and said it was OK. In some cases, less is more. He told Wendy she knew her pet better than anyone else, as long as she kept an eye on me.

I've been on that dosage ever since. My yearly check-ups show I'm in perfect health. That just shows that people must trust their instincts. I'm grateful Mom did.

19
Life Goes On

It was May. We still missed Li'l Tyke. The voice that once told Wendy, "I'll be back as soon as I can," returned to say, "I'm back."

We noticed a sign at our pet store, Petmania in Burbank.

Bottle feeding needed for incoming homeless kittens, the sign read.

Wendy thought that sounded like fun. She thought it would help us get over our grief at losing Li'l Tyke, so she left her name and contact information.

She received a phone call the following morning. "Come get them now, or we're taking them to the shelter."

That was quite a wake-up call! When Wendy walked into the store, the owner pointed toward a tiny crate. Inside was what looked like a blob of black fur, six kittens, each one the size of my paw, only two or three days old.

Wendy was taken aback. She hadn't expected anything quite like that. They looked so tiny and fragile.

"Take the crate home with you," the owner said.

"Take them home? I thought I'd bottle feed them here."

"Nope."

She brought them home. The shop gave her supplies and told her what to do, but she had never done that before. The youngest kitty she ever had was her first one, Tiger, brought home from a neighbor's house. He was four weeks old. Suddenly she had six kittens, all barely three days old.

As soon as she walked into our house with those tiny creatures Sam and I were beyond curious. We sniffed the air as she walked by holding the crate tightly in her arms.

"Yes, we have visitors, Guys," she said.

Marmaladee got up from the couch and eyed the crate. Guernsey May was on the kitchen table, staring, too. Wendy went upstairs and placed the crate on the floor of the closet in the second bedroom. She was being overly protective, but it seemed wise to me. She let us visit a couple at a time so we could introduce ourselves and give the newcomers an inspection.

For the next few days and weeks, we were up around the clock, feeding the little guys. It was all Wendy could do to place the tiny nipple from the bottle into their hungry little mouths. A couple of them took to the nipple easily, but the others had trouble keeping it in.

Besides feeding the kittens, she had to stimulate their genital area to help them do their business. At first, she took them to the sink one at a time, dripped water on them, and they'd pee what little amount they had. Then she fed them. They were all pure black, and, though they were tiny, they could crawl and climb pretty darn well.

After feeding one, she set him into a tall wastepaper basket. Otherwise, she'd never be able to tell them apart back in the crate. That way, she avoided confusion, and everyone had a turn.

Sam and I knew them by scent, but Wendy had her own system. Before putting them back into the crate, she gave them another little dip of water to make sure they were fully relieved.

Within a day of Wendy taking the first kitten out, Sam was right beside her, licking the little one's genital area. He did that with the next one, and so on. He was their official stimulator. The kittens meowed their appreciation, and Sam welcomed the next customer.

I sat and watched in fascination. Wendy let me sniff each one. More often than not I gave them kisses. Hilary and a friend of hers named Suzan came to visit and helped out with the feedings. Suzan loaned us a wonderful, large kitty condo, so as the kittens grew, they'd have plenty of room to run around and climb. She also brought the best cat food anyone could buy.

The kittens grew quickly. One day, Wendy noticed a tiny flash of white on one and said, "Let's call you Flash."

Another had white on his paws, so he was called Mittens. Another had a little white bib, so she was Bib.

We named the runt of the litter Puddin', another little girl Lady Cassandra, and the final kitty had large ears, so he became Yoda. Later, when Yoda was seven weeks old, his legs were so long he was dancing and tripping on the floor, so we added the name Bo Jangles.

Flash and Yoda Bo Jangles were the naughty pair and the leaders of the pack. They were the first to come bounding from their crates, the first to run across the floor to their dinner dishes, and the first to find themselves in some innocent trouble.

Then it hit Wendy that the flash on Flash's back was right where Maxamussy scratched a Z on Elmo's back. Was that a sign?

"I'm back," the voice said.

Could it be that Li'l Tyke orchestrated his return, along with Elmo and Maxamussy? Maybe a bit of them landed in Flash and Yoda Bo Jangles. They had some Burmese in them, so that could account for Li'l Tyke, since he was Siamese, and they all talked a lot. Flash turned out to have diarrhea of the mouth when he grew up. Yoda Bo Jangles looked like a black Siamese and was slick and gorgeous like Maxamussy.

Flash, like Li'l Tyke, had a boy-like quality. Wendy felt if he were a human boy, he'd be a soccer player. Elmo was a total boy, too. I wondered if souls really returned to new bodies. If they did, the situation made plenty of sense. If anything, it was a great comfort to think about it.

I wondered about the voice Wendy heard, too. Was

she going mad? Marmaladee became a surrogate mom, especially with Flash. She bathed him for hours, swatted him for misbehaving, and fell asleep with her paws around him. She tended to the others, too, but she was partial to Flash. I always had a couple kittens burrowing into my hair, trying to get as close as possible. I put up with it but gave Wendy a look that asked, *Do I have to?*

Often, I gently moved away, and the event repeated. I was flattered, but I wasn't a mommy. Puddin' was the first to find a home, then Bib, then finally Lady Cassandra.

Wendy was told she could keep one of the kittens. Her heart was stolen the moment she saw Flash, so that was a no-brainer. However, his best friend Yoda Bo Jangles, had gotten under our skin. We didn't want to separate them, so we didn't.

Our household was more than complete. Sam and I had five kitties to look after. I took over being the caregiver of the kitties, kissing them every day whether they liked it or not. I found myself calmer on our walks. Maybe the kittens helped and got me interested in something else. I was in my zone, sniffing everything, and I began greeting people and their dogs with joyful whimpers. That was new.

Hilary and Wendy couldn't get over the change in me. It took seven years. Wasn't that the time for completion? I thought all the different activities, like bringing other critters into our home, gave me joy.

We occasionally boarded friends' dogs. We took care of two Maltese's, Captain Jack and Nikko. Chewey had more fun playing with them. Our favorite was Jasper, a black Cocker Spaniel. He fit in like clockwork each time he stayed with us. He also befriended Flash. The two of them cuddled up together. Jasper gave him a good wash. It was a harmonious home, and everyone was happy. Savannah would have been proud.

A favorite house/pet sitting job we had was with the "Corgi Clan." One of Wendy's best friends, Scott, had a Corgi named Kevin. He was a handsome, sweet and gentle boy. Actually I had a little crush on him. Don't tell Sam! Scott also had two cats, Squeal and Stella, that we cared for. I didn't become as close to them as I did with Kevin. He always made me feel so comfortable. He loved chasing and retrieving his toys. I couldn't care less, but I ran after him anyway to join in the fun. They had a lovely backyard with a lush lawn. I loved how it felt under my paws.

One day Scott brought home a little puppy he named Cathy. She was actually Kevin's niece. They came from the same breeder. Cathy grew into a feisty little girl with a lot to say. She took charge over everyone, and she'd let you know with her silly little growl. She didn't mean any harm. It was just her way of communicating. I liked her. Sam, Kevin, Cathy, and I were fast friends. We stayed at Scott's house sometimes for a week while he was out of town and had many long walks together. It was a mini-vacation for all of us.

Unfortunately, in November 2008, Scott discovered Kevin had cancer. Our last stay with him, Wendy was giving him several medications throughout the day. We all prayed the chemo would work, but Kevin died on January 13th just 2 weeks after our last visit. He was only six. We had a nice ceremony for him up at Scott's ranch in Santa Ynez where he is buried under a beautiful tree. I miss that boy.

Scott decided to have Cathy bred, to keep Kevin's lineage in the family. Cathy gave birth to several puppies, but only one little guy survived. "Josh" was adorable. Cathy, the proud mom, allowed Sam and me to give him sniffs and love. Soon he was bounding about, getting into mischief like any healthy puppy.

Once Josh was old enough, he, along with Cathy and Sam, who joined in just for the fun of it, went into doggie training with Wendy's trainer friend Sha. The mom and son weren't too thrilled about the discipline they were learning but went along with it. I can't blame them. I don't see the point in it, but Sam was a big help. He obeyed and aced everything. I think Josh and Cathy watched him and eventually copied him. They all graduated with honors.

One very hot summer weekend all of us went to Scott's and his friend's ranch in Santa Ynez. I love the smell of horses. I'd hang out with them, but they are really big and intimidate me a little.

Our friends Michele and John joined us with their beautiful Border Collie "BeBe." We first met BeBe when Michele brought her home as a wee puppy. My goodness! I've never known such energy coming from a dog. This was a new experience for me. I tried to keep up with her, but I just couldn't! Sam and BeBe had a lot of fun together. They went on big hikes into the mountains. Sam told me all about it when he came home before he took a really long nap.

The first morning at the ranch, Wendy put her bathing suit on and told us we were going for an adventure. I couldn't wait to find out where we were going.

We took a nice walk until we reached the Santa Ynez River, right at the border of the ranch. Wendy and the others carried big rubber tubes. Once we got to the river, both Cathy and Josh, like professional swimmers, jumped straight into the water. I took my time getting in, but once I was in, I swam with glee!

The last time I went swimming was in the Baghdad Palace pool! As I swam in the river, I thought of my life back then compared to what it is now, it's unbelievable. It is definitely a totally different lifetime. I don't want to even remember those days, but they are such a part of me that sometimes it is hard to forget. I simply remind myself that I am safe and loved, and I love everything about my life now. I have so much to be grateful for. When I think this way it helps to let those bad sensations go. After all, we dogs are supposed to live in the present. So that's what I do.

Sam, like Savannah did, keeps me in check all the time. Sam. Where is he? Then I saw him still standing on the riverbank, just staring at me with great concern. He began to cry. I told him to jump in, but then he began to bark. Wendy tried gently to persuade him to join us, but he would have nothing to do with touching the water. As soon as his ankles were wet, he'd jump backward to the shore. He was petrified. I thought all Labradors loved water! Sam was part Lab and maybe Husky or Shepherd. I was surprised he was so scared. He's always been my warrior hero. I felt bad for him, but the water felt so good to me.

I did my doggie paddle and could feel my muscles relax. Wendy picked me up and sat me down on her stomach as she sat back into the big black rubber tube. Suddenly we were moving, floating down the river. Everyone was laughing and having so much fun. This was a first for me, and I could see myself doing this a lot! I loved how we bounced about, splashing the water into our faces, cooling us all down from the hot sun.

Meanwhile Sam was crying and barking as he followed us downriver. He refused to walk along the base of the river which was only about two inches of water. Instead he was in the thick, swampy brush. By the time we made it to the end, Sam was filthy, covered in mud. We all had to slip and slide through the muddy edge to get up to dry land. I thought "Let's do it again!" We almost did, but the others decided it was time for lunch. I will never forget this day. I will treasure it forever.

On May 5, 2015 Wendy received a phone call from Scott. Suddenly Cathy became gravely ill and passed overnight. This was a shock to everyone. She, like her Uncle Kevin, was only six.

When I visited Josh, I nestled up to him to give him love, sensing his devastated loss. He told me he couldn't understand what happened. He never got to say goodbye, never sensing her decline. I comforted him the best I could. I know it meant a lot to him. I couldn't imagine losing my mom like that. However, I hardly knew my mom. Now Cathy is buried next to her Uncle Kevin at the ranch under that beautiful tree. We will always have such wonderful memories of being together.

20

More Growing Pains

On September 21, 2011, Wendy's beautiful darling mum passed away. That meant a tremendous change in our lives. Gini's little four-legged family, Chewey and Sterling would need a new home. We inherited both animals. Wendy knew it would be a challenge, because Chewey hadn't gotten over his Napoleon complex. We needed to be on guard every minute. He had to be crated whenever we left.

It worked, though Sam and I felt terrible, because he cried. Then one day, when we were hanging around the house, we all must have looked away for a moment, and a fight began. Sam was no longer being a nice guy, because Chewey's teeth hurt him. Sam retaliated and bit Chewey above the eye, making the eye pop out. He was a Terrier mix with Lhasa Apso, a breed prone to eye conditions.

Wendy rushed him off to the vet, and Chewey's eye was saved, thank Goodness. Wendy decided Chewey needed another home. It wasn't fair for all of us to live in constant fear. I hated losing a playmate, but I was nervous a lot, too. I knew Chewey couldn't be trusted.

Wendy contacted The Rescue Train, a dog and cat rescue group to help with the adoption. They had beautiful photos made of Chewey, and Wendy created a good flyer. She met several people who fell in love with Chewey, but he was miserable and acted out by peeing everywhere. Also, the people all commented how Chewey was so attached to Wendy. When she was around, his behavior was totally different.

She cried over the situation for many nights. Even when Chewey lived with Gini, whenever we visited, when it was time to leave, Gini had to drag Chewey back inside her house. Chewey wanted to jump in the car with us.

We knew how much he loved Wendy, and he kept telling me he wanted to be with us, but I told him that unless he could behave himself with Sam, it wouldn't happen. Chewey refused to talk with Sam. Sam tried his best to reach a truce, telling him he liked him, but Chewey wouldn't have it.

What did Wendy have to do? The answer was to be even more vigilant. He ended up staying with us. Surprisingly, the situation at the house slowly improved. Sam made a point of giving Chewey his space, and maybe the eye episode taught Chewey something.

I was thrilled to have my two buddies. I was happy about everything in those days. Sam, Chewey, and I made another good friend when Hilary adopted a beautiful Lhasa Apso named Nigel. It was great having him so close. We took nightly walks together, and I showed

Nigel our special haunts. I walked even more proudly and showed more confidence.

I know the following might sound unbelievable, but it's true. Whoever said, "When it rains, it pours," had a good reason.

In the fall of 2012, Zina Bethune, the founder and owner of Bethune Theatredanse, was killed in a freak accident. Without her, the company Wendy worked for during the last seventeen years couldn't survive. Her classes completely folded.

Wendy went in for a routine eye exam, and four hours later, after seeing two different specialists as an emergency, she was told she might have a melanoma in her right eye. She'd been legally blind in that eye all her life. At first, they agreed it was melanoma, then they changed their prognosis and decided to keep a close watch on her.

She spent two years having the tumor examined at the Jules Eye Institute. Luckily, she was on a full scholarship. Since she had the condition all her life, she wasn't that concerned about it.

Still, that was a scary thing to live through. In December, a client she'd been working with for a couple years died suddenly. She was blind, and Wendy was her assistant with everyday needs and walked her guide dog Doc. Sam and I walked with Doc and Wendy every Wednesday. He was a sweet, fun guy. We all grew very close, and it was a terrible loss.

In January, 2013, another class Wendy taught with the Academy for the Blind was canceled. She'd been working as an account executive for a scrap metal company for a few years, but that business wasn't doing well, and it went bankrupt within a year.

Wendy made some royalties from her song writing of the previous year, but that wouldn't last much longer. Suddenly, she was unemployed. To add to an already dismal situation, the townhouse where we lived needed serious electrical repairs and there were on-going water leaks. It could be dangerous. The landlord had been putting off repairs for a couple of years, saying he couldn't afford to hire the contractors.

This is when Wendy suspected there was mold in the walls because the leaks had been there for several years. She was right. I could smell it, and poor Guernsey May used to hide in a closet that had mold, and she got a terrible skin condition from it. The landlord refused to hire a mold specialist, and Wendy eventually had to pay for it herself.

She also paid for an HVAC inspection to clean out the air system. The company found dangerous mold. The landlord fought her on all of it but grudgingly hired a company to clear out the mold. Instead of paying our rent the following month, Wendy deducted what she paid, which was even more than the rent payment. The landlord took us to court and won! No one could believe it.

Wendy stated that she was a landlord, too, because she inherited her mother's condo but the judge's mind was made up. Wendy was devastated. We were homeless—with three dogs and six kitties.

That lasted for eight months. What could we do? Wendy looked to me for courage and strength. She told me that after what I went through, she didn't think most people would have lasted as long as I did. They would have given up.

She refused to give up, either. Somehow, we'd make it. She held me every night, saying our prayers together. Sam and Chewey lay quietly beside us. We began packing, putting things into storage. Wendy was fortunate that she was leasing her condo, so she earned enough money to pay for the storage unit and food, but she couldn't afford to live there.

Friends graciously came to our rescue. Wendy began sleeping at three different friends' houses, but she had to foster us out. That broke all our hearts, but there was little we could do. Laurie, our dog trainer, who owned Training with Love for Canines, took Sam and me. Chewey went to live with Gini's wonderful caregiver Walter. He and his family loved Chewey and would have kept him, but they already had ten dogs, and Chewey picked on one of them.

The naughty twins, Flash and Yoda Bo Jangles, went to a friend named Philippe, who Wendy stayed with part-time. Marlamadee, Guernsey May, Cleo, and Sterling went to a lady named Dawn who had a kitty rescue and pet shop called Healthy Paws Store in Whittier, California.

She put them up for six months. That was very generous of her and we will never forget it.

We were blessed, and all of Wendy's and our gratitude will never end for the help we received.

I did my best to comfort Wendy during those days with plenty of attention. What we didn't know was how badly her health was deteriorating and how severely depressed she was.

During the past ten years, Wendy dealt with a diabolical family situation which would have depressed anyone. She became partially financially responsible for Gini. Wendy had to keep going. She couldn't afford to take a break.

All that took a terrible toll on her. It was no wonder she fell apart. Her spirit was broken. I related to her so much, and I sensed the pain and severity of it all. She came to an abyss where she wanted to end it all.

Suddenly she saw Guernsey May's face staring at her bigger than life. Seconds later, my face appeared, my eyes penetrating her vision.

Wendy froze. She hadn't thought of that. Who would take care of her babies? What would we do without her?

She snapped out of it and told us, "You babies are saving my life. Your spirits are so strong! Who's rescuing whom? Thank you, Liberty Pearl and Guernsey May."

That happened at the end of July, 2013. We became homeless the first week of September. Again, our life was turned upside down and changed forever.

21

Don't Give Up

On December 12, 2013, Wendy fell gravely ill and was in the hospital for emergency surgery. She was a walking dead person. She had her appendix out and a complete stomach reconstruction, an ileectomy, they called it.

Meanwhile, Sam, Chewey, and I were already at Philippe's house when the emergency happened. He couldn't keep us, so that's when Sam and I went to our dog trainer Laurie's house, and Chewey went to Gini's caregiver, Walter.

It was hard for Sam and me to stay in a crate at night, but we got used to it. We hung out and played with several dogs.

Sam wasn't himself. He was very agitated, missing Wendy. I was OK, as long as I was with Sam, but I was very concerned for him during those days. We had a lovely Christmas. Laurie gave us each a stocking full of goodies. She was so kind to us.

Wendy was down to ninety-three pounds, losing thirty pounds overnight. The doctors told her it would be two years before she'd feel herself again, and they were right. While still staying at three different friends' homes, she went back to the emergency clinic for a few days every month until September, 2014.

Even with all of that and being separated from us, she said she was blessed. First, she was alive. The doctors at the hospital told her they were amazed she was still walking and hadn't died. She overcame horrible odds.

"Didn't you overcome horrible odds, too?" she asked me. "You survived being at the Baghdad Palace when it blew up. Bombs fell everywhere. How did you survive? You had a concussion and were completely shell shocked. It took years of unconditional love and constant encouragement for you to be a dog, free and happy. If you can fight your way through unbelievable stress, then so can I."

Wendy said I had an amazing spirit and I was a perfect example of spirit overcoming anything and everything. It wouldn't be easy for her, but with all the love around Wendy from her dear friends and her critters, she'd be back. We'd make sure of it.

It was clear that I inspired her. I don't want to sound conceited, but she told me about it all the time. Every day in the hospital and for the following two years, when her body was struggling to heal, she looked at me and marveled. It made me feel embarrassed, but I couldn't hear enough! I was happy my love was helping her.

Months later, once we were all together again, we had conversations during our nightly love-ins. Our life was put on hold. She wrote a musical, *Love, Larry,* and a cookbook titled *Straight From the Horse's Mouth!* Yes, that was a "Mister Ed" cookbook. Wendy's dad, Angus, was known as Alan Young who played Wilbur on the '60s popular TV show. She also started my story, but all those were set aside for a while.

She swore I was sent to her as her little savior. I gave her many answers. During one of our love-in sessions, while looking straight into my big brown eyes, a voice spoke, and it was mine.

"Don't give up your dreams," I told her. "Keep seeing your dreams."

She didn't expect that. It reminded her of what the wonderful actress Betty White once said to her in 2001. Wendy met Betty at a memorial for the actress and their friend, Kathleen Freeman. Wendy was representing a script written by her friend, Deborah Hand-Cutler, which she gave to Betty. Betty loved it and offered to go to the producer's table with it. Because of the demographics at the time, it couldn't be sold. Producers said Betty White couldn't sell lemonade.

Betty asked Wendy how the script was doing, and Wendy told her the ridiculous excuse the producers gave her.

"Don't ever lose that dream," Betty said. "Keep seeing that dream."

My words reminded Wendy that she'd keep getting

stronger and would eventually bounce back. Wendy was determined.

I also gave her a sense of humor. My little antics were adorable, I had to admit. Just my expression could make her laugh. When I made her laugh, I rolled on my back and wiggled back and forth, smiling to say, "I got you!"

In early March, 2014, Wendy's friend, Jayne, fostered Marmaladee and Guernsey May. Jayne recently lost her cat named Yoda and welcomed the purring company of our girls. We still miss them, but we know they're loved, and so is Jayne. Wendy visits when she can, which takes the sting of the loss away a little.

She found another lovely foster home with Ramos, who cared for Cleo and Sterling. Ramos fell in love with Sterling, who is still with her. Cleo and the twins eventually made it back to us, but it was later than anyone expected.

❧

Another dear friend, Ed, couldn't stand to see us living as we were. One night when Wendy didn't have a place to go, because she didn't want to overdo her welcome at her friends' homes after seven months of living with them, she told Ed she would sleep in her car.

Ed laughed. "Wendy, you don't have a car."

He was right. She forgot. The court ruling from her eviction took her car in possession to pay back the supposed back rent.

Jayne, who took in Marmaladee and Guernsey May, took in another stray for two nights—Wendy.

Flash and Yoda Bo Jangles were staying with Philippe. Flash was quite the talker. It would probably drive most people nuts, but not Wendy or any of us critters. We loved it. He had a lot to say and used many voices to express himself. We found it fascinating, and Wendy had deep conversations with him. Yoda Bo Jangles had more of the Siamese physically, where Flash had the narrative talent.

Flash's talking greatly disturbed Philippe.

"Can't you train him to shut up?" Philippe asked. "I can't think."

Wendy felt bad for him. Philippe had his own technique for making Flash shut up, which we had to admit helped. He said, "Shhhiiit," not the swear word but by barely pronouncing the *t* and using a *d* instead, with a lot of stress on the sh. That made Flash stop for at least two minutes. Still, I was sure Philippe also said the swear word many times out of frustration, but Flash was determined to speak his mind.

It was more than time for all of our clan to find a place to live, back together again.

22

Home Sweet Home

Wendy and Ed negotiated a deal so we could rent a home. Wendy's attorney drew up an agreement for a certain amount of money as a loan against her condo. We found the perfect house in Woodland Hills. Amazingly, the landlord accepted Wendy and approved us. Actually it was just us three dogs and three kitties, Flash, Yoda Bo Jangles and Cleo.

Jayne offered to hold onto Marmaladee and Guernsey May until we could bring them home later, once Wendy was more settled. Wendy didn't feel too guilty, because they were being loved and well taken care of, though we missed them badly. Marmaladee was my kitty, after all. And in March of 2017 we were all thrilled when we had Marmaladee stay with us for a week. It was like the old days. She was really happy to see us. She slept by Wendy's side. We made sure to move over and give her plenty of space.

The house was perfect, and we were very happy. We had a large, lovely backyard. Wendy loved watching me run through the green grass, my tail and head high, feeling the breeze on my face. Sam, Chewey, and I settled into the new sounds of the neighborhood with a few barks occasionally when the mailman came, or when strangers knocked on the door. At night before we went to sleep I made a ritual of washing Cleo's face and neck. How she puts up with me I don't know, but she does. It's our thing now.

I always began the chorus of *Someone we don't know is here!* I turned into quite a little watchdog. As I mentioned earlier, I was never a cuddler, but suddenly, I surrendered to Wendy. She needed all the love she could get. I nosed her, wanting her to pet me, belly rubs and all for a good loving. Every night, I snuggled up to her before we fell asleep. We were falling more and more in love.

One day, Wendy had a heart-to-heart chat with me. She told me she had to be doing something right, even after the past disastrous eight months. She asked how she deserved us precious, amazing, four-legged souls. She felt honored and blessed that we chose to live with her. She wanted us to know we saved her. She said she never would have gotten through the past few years without us. With us, she had something to live for and take care of.

"It might sound silly, Libby, but you're really taking care of me. Your tenacity, your huge heart, and your courage teach me daily. Each day you showed your amazing strength by being more and more of a dog. That's how it should be, the natural way."

It seemed like Wendy's entire being was focused on enabling me just to be a happy little dog, living my life my own way without drama or fear. She said she had to apply that to her own life, too.

"Libby, here you are, being a happy little dog and so much more. I never asked more from you than what you had to offer. Your possibilities are endless. What a huge lesson for us people. I thank God every day for giving you to me."

I felt touched by our talk. I loved her a lot, so I kissed her all over.

Unfortunately, the owners of the Woodland Hills house had to put it up for sale, so we had to find a new place to live. It came down to a tight crunch, but we found a house within one day of the deadline. We have been here for over three years now with an even bigger yard.

Sam had always suffered from major separation anxiety, and it got worse after the last move. He became manic when Wendy would leave. He went through two trainings for it, but his neurosis still takes over. He has torn things up in the house, including the plantation shutters, the antique chairs, an air-conditioning hose, and even the front door jamb.

Wendy tried crating him, but he chewed through the steel crate several times, even after repairs, and he broke a tooth. She tried Benadryl, then doggie Prozac, but that was like giving him water. We have a chain-link dog run that's totally secure in the backyard, but he has managed to uproot the six-inch pegs that were added for more security around the base.

Wendy tried keeping him outside with a secured fence, but he became a Houdini and escaped through the tiniest holes. Then one day Wendy's friend, Jaynee, came over with her drill, hammer, and nails and built fencing that looked like something made by the Gestapo. Sam *still* wedged through a tiny hole near the fencing, so more fencing was added to run all along the wooden fence.

I would ask him "Why are you freaking out?" I tried to figure out what was going on in his head. I tried to calm him down, but he would be hysterical. I realized I had to stay out of his way.

We did finally "de-Samitize," and Sam is getting used to the backyard, though he still goes under the house and peeks out through the bricks, as Wendy drives away. It may be that after her surgery, he feels the urgency of her care needs. He's been her service dog for the past few years after proving his ability to nurse her.

When Wendy was recuperating from surgery, he steadied her up and down stairs and stayed close whenever she walked. He was truly amazing, and we knew it was separation anxiety. It was better after we had two roommates living with us. They're home most of the time, working out of the house, so Sam has company to keep him calm.

Being raised in a shelter got him accustomed to having people around 24/7.

Wendy keeps Chewey and me in Sam's old, large crate whenever she leaves. This is for our own safety, as Sam and Chewey sometimes still fight. Wendy was on disability for the past four years and probably will stay on it a bit longer. We're all taking baby steps.

Over two years ago, she started a part-time job as a special needs helper. She seems cut out for that work. She could bring Sam with her. I tell her to keep seeing her dreams every day, which is why she decided to finish my story. That's one dream accomplished.

23

Taking Care of One Dream, Losing Another

On Thursday, May 19, 2016, Wendy awoke with the overwhelming urge to start my story again. She hadn't looked at it in years. She dived into the part about Savannah on June 3, the day before she died. It was grueling getting through those moments, but she did it. The next day, Friday, May 20, around four o'clock, she finished writing about our beloved girl's passing, then she set the story aside, feeling depleted of emotion after reliving her final moments with her.

She turned on the TV for the four o'clock news. Her friend, Bobbi Jo called.

"I'm so sorry to hear about your daddy," Bobbi Jo said.

Wendy's stomach tightened. "Oh, no. Is he gone?"

"Yes. I'm very sorry. He died yesterday, the nineteenth."

We looked up at the tv screen and there was the headline, *Alan Young Dies at 96*. The story continued, showing clips of him with Mister Ed and giving other information.

She was stunned. Her older siblings had plotted to keep Wendy from seeing her daddy for the last several years, and never told her he was dying or that he had passed. Her dad knew how much she loved him, and she knew he loved her. I missed seeing him, and Sam never got to know him.

🐾

The dream of being with him again never came true. We had to let it go. I really loved him. He was always happy to see me and Savannah, though I felt Savannah was his favorite.

As always, at night before going to sleep, we went through the day's journey together. During the rough days after her daddy's passing, I looked at her with what she called my big brown soulful eyes full of love, saying, *It's all right, Mummy. All is well.*

In September, 2016, our precious Guernsey May passed over the Rainbow Bridge. Eight months later, in May, 2017, our li'l Cleo followed. Wendy decided to rescue some kitties in their names. I loved the idea as I had so much fun when we were fostering all those dogs and the kittens.

We went to a shelter where we found a beautiful nine-year old Siamese girl named Betty who was on the red list. Wendy immediately changed her name to Beauty and we found her a lovely home within a week. I wished we had kept her. She was so gentle.

That same week we fell in love with a 3-legged, deaf

and partially blind kitty we named "Puddin'." We took her in, planning to keep her. She was a real love-bug, giving kisses all the time. She licked me every night before we went to sleep.

That same weekend Wendy met a gal who had just found a five-day old kitten under a bush. The mother never returned. Wendy agreed to bottle feed the baby. Puddin' took a real liking to her and took over all cleaning duties. The two would play and sleep in each others' arms. I was fascinated. I remember when Flash and Yoda Bo Jangles were that tiny but you forget how fragile they are.

Unfortunately, because of Puddin' being deaf and partially blind, she would freak out when we dogs walked or ran up beside her. She actually began attacking us. One day she went after Sam. Sam is way too big and Wendy was afraid something could happen. So, with tears, we returned Puddin' to the rescue group.

Later that summer we rescued two beautiful Tuxedo kitties that were to be euthanized that day for "behavior" reasons. Well, they turned out to be the sweetest kitties. "Tucker" found a home that same day he was rescued and "Donovan" has his forever home with Wendy's good friend Alex.

Of course, we kept the kitten Gracee. And, by the way, she announced her name the moment Wendy met her! She became the ruler of the household. She is quite a character and loves her Uncle Flash. Chewey and Gracee play hide and seek. I can't be bothered, I just watch them, betting on Gracee to win.

24

Life Simply Is

It's June 4, 2018, and I'm fifteen and a half years old. I moved in with Wendy and the clan over fourteen years ago. Where has the time gone? Savannah passed ten years ago. Wendy can't help thinking how proud Savannah would be of me. We like to think of her busting her buttons, so to speak, lovingly and protectively hovering over me.

Savannah, you did an amazing job. Look at me now! I'm healthy, bright, and one of the happiest dogs ever. I'm the first to bark if someone comes to the door. I'm the leader of the pack, though I let Sam think he is.

Wendy says my happy disposition shows itself every day, and I'm such a comedienne. I'm not aware of that. I've taken to talking a bit, too, especially when the TV is on. I know when the commercials are playing, because Wendy gets up or uses the remote to fast forward. I walk up to her, and, in my finest voice, let out a "Well" that stretches into a growly yawn. I flip on my back and begin squirming back and forth. The floor has magical, massaging fingers that give me the perfect rubdown, while I sigh and groan in ecstasy.

When the commercial is over, and the program resumes, I jump on the couch and lie close to Wendy, snuggling for an ear and head massage. That's our nightly routine. I still have my Percorten shot every six weeks and Prednisone every other day for Addison's. Unfortunately, my long, flowy hair over my head has disappeared. I don't miss it, but Wendy does. Either it stopped growing from the cortisone affecting my hair growth or from the time the groomer cut all my hair off, much to Wendy's shock, because she didn't ask her to do that. A Coton de Tulear should never be shaved like that.

Other than showing a cataract in my left eye, I'm in great shape. Marcy and others expressed concern that I wouldn't live long due to the stress in my early life, but Wendy wasn't concerned.

People often say, "Love conquers all," and I was a testament to that. We're very fortunate and grateful. Sam has a lot to do with it. He was amazing the way he took over Savannah's job, though Sam doesn't see it as a job. Chewey has become my best playmate. He allows me to be dominant. I love my family.

When we go to bed, all of us dogs jump onto the bed with Wendy. We play "The cookie fairy" game of Wendy hiding the cookies under her pillow and her pretending not to know. Then she exclaims "Oh! The cookie fairy came" and we all have our treats.

Sam cuddles up under her right arm, but I manage to squeeze in between them, or I end up on her chest.

Chewey is on her left side. Then there's Flash, who always ends up on her pillow, leaning his bum against her head. Gracee snuggles in wherever she can. Cleo and Yoda Bo Jangles greet us at the bedroom door first thing in the morning.

Every day, Wendy asks each of us, "Have I told you lately how much I love you?"

No answer is needed or expected. It's always the same—love is reflected all around us. Wendy used to pray about Savannah when she was three or four, asking the universe to please let her live until she reached eight or ten. When she hit seven, Wendy prayed she'd reach ten or twelve. At eleven, she prayed for twelve to fourteen, and at thirteen, it was fourteen to sixteen.

When sixteen came, Wendy and I were so grateful, we left it up to God or the universe. She made it to almost eighteen. Wendy doesn't do that anymore. It was too much pressure on her heart strings. She certainly doesn't want to add pressure to me.

We just pray that all of us live long, full, healthy lives. Wendy feels that when someone has had many critters in her life and have stared death in the face, you give up holding onto what you want. We can't control anything, so she chooses to just live in the moment like we dogs have taught her. We showed her how to live each moment to the fullest, full of love and happiness. We deal with things as they come, but we always keep a positive outlook. It's what we know.

Wendy says, "You don't know anything else, bless you. You're so about love and are simply living your lives. Your spirits are so free."

All is well and peaceful. We're happy. We're infinitely bonded and thrilled to be sharing this life together.

AFTERWORD

In Closing from Wendy

Liberty Pearl's journey from the Baghdad Presidential Palace will always be a wonder. Who would ever imagine a little puppy surviving bombs exploding all around? She was abandoned and hid in the smoking rubble alone. Then she survived the emotional trauma that so affected her little body. She is a war hero.

I thank all the good people who assisted in her rescue: Our Marines who first found her, Margaret Ledger, and Colonel Susan, for giving her such comfort and love. I thank Marcy Christmas for beginning her mission of re-homing dogs from Iraq, paying for Liberty Pearl's travel and for fostering her for seven months. I also thank Dr. David Schwartz for the best veterinary care, my mum and dad, and all our friends and neighbors who witnessed Libby's amazing growth from a six-pound body of anxious fear into a well-rounded, funny, curious, confident ball of love.

Whether anyone believes in God or not, there was definitely a guardian angel looking out for her. She was meant to be here. I'm so grateful for her. She's the little white dog I always wanted and more. She has given me so much again and again, rescuing me through the most trying time of my life. Sure, I took care of her, but not like the way she took care of me. I pray she remains healthy and lives a long, full life. So far, we're doing really well, thank heaven. She's fifteen and a half now!

Liberty Pearl, you made this happen. In your own little self, you created life with such courage, having the strongest will to live and expressing abundant spirit and love. That is the gift you gave me. We have everything we need right here and now. Who could ask for anything more?

Liberty Pearl

Libby and Sam

Sterling

Marmaladee's visit.

Sam   Chewey

Chewey, Libby & Sam

Puddin'   *Donovan*

Flash   *Yoda Bo Jangles*

Tucker

Beauty "Betty"

Yoda Bo Jangles & Flash, aka "The Naughty Twins"

Gracee

Libby & Gracee

Thank you for reading my story! Liberty Pearl

In Memory of our beloved kitties who passed during the completion of this book.

Sweetest Guernsey May. May 22, 2001 – Sept. 10, 2016

Our li'l heart Cleo. 2000 – May 21, 2017

Our precious Sterling. 1999 – June 17, 2018

ABOUT THE AUTHOR

Wendy is a first-time author, but a published song-writer. She has written her first musical.

Wendy began her career at age 10, as a ballerina with The Bolshoi Ballet and later performed on Broadway and in London, England. She taught the performing arts to special-needs children and adults for 18 years.

She lives in Los Angeles with her four-legged clan.